MORE THAN A MIRACLE

MORE THAN A MIRACLE

By

CHINWE EZEANYA

To Princess Ndidi Mbanugo.
With Compliments.
Chinwe.
1/1/19.

origami

Parrésia Publishers Ltd. .
82, Allen Avenue, Ikeja, Lagos, Nigeria.
+2348154582178, +2348062392145
origami@parresia.com.ng
www.parresia.com.ng

ISBN: 978-978-55743-9-5

Printed in Nigeria by Parrésia Press

This book is dedicated to God Almighty, the Miracle Giver, Dr. Jesus: My Master and Friend.

To my dear husband Mike, for his labour of love and for ensuring our son Dike was saved by single-handedly taking care of all his medical bills during our journey through Dike's medical challenge.

Also to our daughters Ugonna, Amaka and especially Dalu, the baby of the house prior to Dike's birth, who only got a fraction of our time as we were engrossed in the battle to save Dike's life.

To all my new (extended liver transplant family) especially Zaheera and Azhar; Bella and Hawaii; Salimatu and Ahmed; Manenka and Evelyn Etta; Chinedu and Ugochukwu Obiakor; Medya Musungu; the Mayakis and many others.

You are all Giants in my life.

‘Life is mostly froth and bubble. Two things stand like stone.
Kindness in another’s trouble and courage in our own.’

– Adam Gordon

All scriptural references are from the open source version of the King James Version available online at https://www.biblegateway.com.

CONTENTS

ACKNOWLEDGMENTS

I owe my greatest gratitude to God for blessing me with a great family, friends, church and numerous well-wishers. I would specially thank...

Pastor E. A. Adeboye (Daddy G.O.), Pastor Alaye Ogan, and all the numerous pastors, the choir and congregation of the parishes of RCCG, House Fellowship Centers, RCCG Bible School, the Charismatic Movement of the Sacred Heart Cathedral New Delhi and the pastors and congregation of Christ Church Port-Harcourt, who upheld us in prayers especially during the first two years of Dike's life.

I would like to thank Dr. A. S. Soin, Dr. Neelam Mohan, their team of Liver Transplant Specialists and the entire staff of Sir Ganga Ram Hospital and Medanta Hospital in New Delhi, for allowing God use them to achieve our miracle. Also for their devotion to saving lives, breaking new grounds in the field of medicine and giving hope to many.

To Haresh and Priya Ahuja whom God directed to us to enable the celebration of our loved ones. I also acknowledge all those who conceived the idea of a possible liver donation notably Rumundaka and Dr. Chizoba Wonodi, Uzo Chuma, Tonye Cole, Emmanuel Arinze, Ritchie Emeni, Mummy Meg Molokwu, Dame Adeline, Anyanna Imoke, Zaheera, Maresh and Kiran Jejhani. You all are my everyday heroes.

I would like to thank all my family members and extended families of Ezeanya, Ikokwu, Cole, Offor, Ibe, Nwazota, Nwosu, Wonodi, Obinwa, Arinze, Molokwu, Ike, Adimora and Chuma-Okoli, who supported us in different ways in the course of our turbulent years. Thank you for being there for us always.

To Tonye and Sylvia Cole for their love and support, especially for the numerous calls and advice.

My special thanks goes to Dr. Uzo Awogu, Prof. Ifeoma Egbuonu, Mrs. Lolo Ibeanusi, Dr. Ekeoku, Dr. Gbobo, Dr. Ahmed, Dr. Uju Bosah, Dr. Otubelu, Dr. Nseobong Undie, Dr. Sidney Ibeanusi and all their team members; and to all other doctors too numerous to mention who assisted us in various ways from Dike's birth till date.

To my Sisters in Christ who took care of my family while we were away in India: Onyekachi Uduku, Chinenye Uwakwe and Sharon Adebola. Special thanks also to my Aunt and birthday mate Dame Adeline Nwazota and my friends Ugochukwu and Ebere Mbaegbu (BFF) for their sacrifice of love to have spent over three months each with us in India.

To Dike's God-parents who continue to stand by us in prayers and support: Dike Ibe, Professor Ideriah and Chika Peterside.

To Chief and Dr. Mrs. Alexis Ajuebon, who have stood by us as mentors and pillars in all our endeavours. To my professional colleagues, friends and acquaintances too numerous to mention, who have eagerly upheld us in their prayers and cheered Dike on in their excitement of witnessing the proof of a living miracle.

To Nkoyo Eze who assisted with the book editing and especially to Ngozi Toks Osu for working tirelessly under pressure as my Literary Consultant to edit and package this book. And to Azafi Omoluabi-Ogosi of Parresia Publishers for publishing Dike's story.

Thank you all for being part of our miracle. It's really been More Than A Miracle.

FOREWORD

It's my pleasure to write a foreword for this book, *More Than A Miracle* written by Chinwe Ezeanya.

Dike's story convinces you of miracles! Chinwe is truly a charismatic personality and I have fond memories of my interaction with her. We knew Dike needed a liver transplant but sadly there was no matching donor in the family despite everyone who was willing to donate, and even his mom who was willing did not have a matching blood group. I did request her to go back home eventually after waiting for several months, as it seemed we had no hope. One thing intrigued me a lot about her; she would consistently say, "I believe in my Lord and I know you will be the healer and will cure my child"; I don't know how?!

It sounded vague/funny as it was the family who had to come out with a live related donor as we didn't have a sound cadaveric donation programme in our country and an international patient would definitely not get this opportunity.

One fine day, I suddenly got this idea - why can't we swap donors to benefit two needy patients? This had never been done before in India and it needed a large surgical team for four people to be operated on simultaneously (two patients and two donors).

After selecting the right swap donors and patients, we performed the surgery having taken permission from Government. Thereafter, the news of this breakthrough surgery was as rampant as wild fire in our country, both in the papers and electronic media, besides international coverage, *"Liver unites families across continents"*. This was the first Swap Liver Transplant in India and it paved way for several others to follow thereafter. What would you call this? It was this utmost faith of Chinwe that led me to think "out of the box" and end up with a miraculous saving of Dike.

The blessings of Dike's family and several others have resulted in my achieving the highest award in medicine in India called the BC Roy National Award by the Indian President.

I'm fortunate that the Lord chose me to be the healer which Chinwe could foresee!

Liver unites families across continents

INDIAN COUPLE swap livers with Nigerian mother-son duo for transplantation in city

Dike has done so well for himself in all spheres of life and I am truly proud of him. I would take the opportunity to congratulate Mom for her conviction and ability to save her loveable son.

Dr. Neelam Mohan
Director Department of Pediatric Gastroenterology,
Hepatology & Liver Transplantation
Medanta The Medicity Hospital – Gurgaon, India.

INTRODUCTION

More than a Miracle is an emotional and heart-rending story of a mother's love for her son, and ferocity in which we would go to any length to save someone we love. It is a story of trials and triumphs, but mostly of faith; of believing that no matter the situation or the circumstance, God has a way of pulling one through if we firmly believe and trust in Him. It is a story of hope and love – for life, family, friends, and God.

More than a Miracle is written in the first person – a narration by Chinwe Ezeanya – whose son, Dike was born with a congenital liver disease which was misdiagnosed at birth.

Born on 7th January 2008, Dike always looked jaundiced, however when he was about 3 months old, a trusted consultant paediatrician discovered the source of his illness and he was ultimately referred to a hospital in India for proper diagnosis and cure. They went to India, and the solution was a liver transplant.

It is usually advised that donors for liver transplants are family as they are the closest match, although the transplant is only done if the donor agrees to give a part of his liver. Unfortunately, Dike's father had recently had surgery so he wasn't considered a healthy fit. And his mother, Chinwe has a different blood type so she wasn't considered a match either. It seemed Dike had a death sentence.

Chinwe and her son moved to India in search of a medical solution. During the 5 months of waiting, she watched her son's health deteriorate slowly and painfully. He began to show symptoms of the end stages of the disease. Liver cirrhosis had set in and nothing could be done but a transplant. Seeing their dilemma, the Indian doctor proffered a solution – a swap transplant: they find a family who also needs a liver transplant and swap livers. This means, the healthy persons from different families, donate their liver to the sick person of the other family. This had never been done, and was unheard of. It sounded unbelievable but would save Dike's life – if they find a matching family on time.

At some point, the paediatric liver consultant who had given them this solution even advised she go home and look after her three daughters. But Chinwe still hoped for a miracle. After almost 6 months of waiting in India, when Dike had turned 18 months, one mismatched donor, blood donation from strangers, near death experiences, and endless praying, they finally got a donor. The swap liver transplant took place; Chinwe donated her liver to a sick Indian woman, and the woman's husband donated his liver to her son Dike.

It was a landmark surgery done in India. Four operations being done simultaneously in the same hospital; parts of two livers being taken from the donors and transplanted into the recipients all at once. It was huge. The 36-member surgical team working on four patients for 36 hours, taking 10-12 hours to work on each patient. This was 25-26th June 2009. The media was in a frenzy and the news was aired around the world, even here in Nigeria (see ThisDay Newspapers of 11th September 2009).

The story give details of what Chinwe went through with her family as they watched Dike's health deteriorate in the first 18 months of his life. The emotional trauma they experienced and the pains they went through as their beautiful only son seemed to live with a death sentence.

She talks about the overwhelming love and support of family, friends, the church and even complete strangers when they moved to India. But she also talks about the naysayers who kept telling her to "take heart" and allow her son die, as it was the "will of God". About the people who did not understand her pain especially those who were close enough to have understood.

She talks about her faith, how she held on to God even when it looked hopeless. About how her faith waivered, almost losing it but how she was able to keep herself on track by constantly reading scripture and praying for a miracle.

She talks about the stress she experienced in her relationship with her husband, the pains they went through as they both struggled to understand their son's ill health. But she also talks about how it brought them closer together, finding their way back to love; the book is dedicated to her husband for the unending love, care, and sacrifice he has made for her and their family.

Today, we are still surprised by the incredible progress science has made in the life of man. Many scientific wonders though are now taken for granted and man has lost the spirit of wonderment for such progress. My mother never forgave science for the invention of the aeroplane because she never could imagine how a machine could fly and carry people all over the world. (She may have been a little afraid of it since she suspected that this machine may one day carry away her son who wanted to be a pilot, not a doctor or lawyer). Recent advancement in technology communications, space probes, etc. no longer engages our imagination. In medicine, progress in treatment techniques no longer make us stop to think – hip and knee replacement surgery is commonplace, so is heart surgery. In our lifetime, we have seen the cloning of Dolly the sheep; the incredible growth of stem cell research and much else that are no longer in the realm of speculation. The growth of artificial intelligence and drone technology, have implications not yet untapped. While humans can cure, they have progressed technology that can also destroy the world in a matter of seconds. But let us not go there. Dike is alive, is computer literate, can play football, video games and a thousand things his grandfather, a technological Neanderthal and neophyte cannot begin to comprehend!!

Dike has brought the wonder of science, through the even greater wonder of God, into our lives. Whenever we read about the progress of medicine we may be enthused, wonder for a minute and move on. When we see Dike, we do not wonder for a minute. We stop. Thank God and science as the thrill of the excitement of his life washes over us as waves after waves of goose pimples reverberate through our body. What Dike has been through, and his presence in our lives, is literarily miraculous. When Jesus said to the cripple, "Take up your bed and walk", that cripple relives that miracle every second for the remaining days of his life. It becomes the substructure on which the cripple's new life is built. So it is with Dike.

In Dike's case, it is not Dike whose life had been saved by the surgeons of the 36-hour operation by 36 doctors, it is ours. Dike does not go about thinking about the operation. He is unaware of it in a physical sense and may sometimes wonder why we see him as a walking miracle. He is just a young boy who has recovered from an illness. To us, he is much more than that. He is the stuff of legends. He is our legend, our inspiration: the source of our strength, the testimony of our faith.

It is personal to us who know him. To others who may hear his story and share our sense of wonderment – they do so momentarily. For us, the wonderment is a never to be forgotten experience, a reminder that we in ourselves are mere mortals and that the supernatural revealed Himself to us in a personal way which we can never forget or repay. Dike has been given a spirit to tolerate our inadequacies as we wonder at our little "god". He goes about doing the things young people of his age do, he will grow up to be a man and would never understand the incandescence of light we see in him.

I presume great sports men have parents, brothers, etc. Mohammed Ali, Hussein Bolt, etc.; members of their family cannot but believe that they have been specially blessed. If they walk with jauntiness in their step, it is probably because these great athletes are their relatives; the world may forever see them as world champions and claim them as such. But those who are family know them, and can claim them more. So we know Dike. We will remain more than grateful that he is one of us. We can tell his story with greater authenticity. But it is not his story we tell. It is our story and God's manifestation therein.

Dike is now a glowing healthy 10-year-old. His mother, Chinwe turns 50 on 29th May 2018 and is also in good health. So she is telling her story. This is her tribute to life.

For Chinwe Ezeanya, her experience and love for her son, Diken'agha Kenechukwu Nadim Yobanna Victory Ezeanya is indeed more than a miracle.

Patrick Dele Cole, OFR
Ngozi Toks Osu, Editor

CHAPTER 1

Diken'agha

I did not ask for him. I was awed the day I went to the hospital in June 2007 with what I thought were symptoms of malaria and the young female gynaecologist told me I was pregnant. I argued with her as I did not think I could be pregnant, but she smiled and gave me reasons to justify her diagnosis.

"First of all, you have been spotting," she said. "You are still within childbearing age and in a stable marriage," she continued as she watched me closely across her desk.

Her explanation got me thinking, and I realised she was right. I was speechless.

She prescribed some medication to help me rest, and advised I return for a pregnancy test in a fortnight. I thought to myself and smiled as I got up to leave the consulting room.

That was the genesis of our son Dike's conception. His father had often fantasized about the birth of a son into our family as we already had three beautiful daughters. Although we were not bound by the tradition where the female child is not appreciated, my husband still felt our joy would be more complete if we had a son.

And pregnant I was. I eventually settled into pregnancy mode which was surprisingly a lot easier than my three previous pregnancies. After due consultations, I was convinced the baby would be born on my elder brother's birthday. I even confided in him that I had a birthday gift for him which would be delivered on that day. He had no clue as to what the gift was until a few months later when I visited him at his home in Lagos; we both prayed it would indeed be a boy.

A few months later, I had a scan during my antenatal clinic and the doctor informed me I was going to have a son. What joy!

"Oh! This lady already has three princesses; thank God this is a boy," he said.

I was truly excited even though I had not wanted to know what my baby's gender was. Although I did not plan nor care about the sex of my children, I recalled that two of my older cousins had advised me to try a few more times to have a male child. They told me that the African man would always tell his wife that he loves their female children but deep down in his heart, he would feel unfulfilled if he did not have a son. They said most women who believed it was okay would later discover, especially when they became menopausal, that a man's needs change with age and he might eventually step out of his marriage to father other children, in search of a male heir.

Although I was not quite ready for the challenge of having another child, I thanked God. As I accepted this bundle of joy with gratitude, I made up my mind to glow in pregnancy; I did and I was blessed with a good appetite for the right kinds of food. Unlike my previous pregnancies, this was an easy one with only the occasional morning sickness. I was grateful to God for the good health I enjoyed.

I was expected to give birth within the first fortnight of January 2008. As it was highly likely I would have another caesarean section like all my previous pregnancies, I told my doctors I would love to have the baby delivered on the 11th of January which was my elder brother Tonye's birthday. Tonye is so special to me; he is my spiritual mentor and a most humble gentleman with great financial discipline and wisdom. It turned out there were two other people who shared that birthday - the wife of the doctor who scanned me on that day and my friend Nkechi Njokanma who expressed her delight when I told her about my pregnancy. She had asked me to ensure the baby would be born on her birthday.

On the 6th of June 2007, our family travelled to Lagos for my cousin Jackie's wedding after which we left for Dubai to spend the first ten days of our summer vacation. I radiated in my pregnancy all through the period. My husband and I even discussed the possibility of my having our baby in the United States but eventually we decided not to as there were new laws dissuading non-citizens from having their babies born in the United States. We believed that God's perfect will for us would come to pass.

Christmas 2007. On Christmas Eve, my husband Mike suggested that we spend part of the Christmas holidays at The Garden City Protea Hotel, Port Harcourt. I remember it was so peaceful. We discussed the names we would give our son. He suggested Dike and we settled for it. The full name "Diken'agha" means "the mighty warrior in battle" or "God the Mighty warrior". He was named after one of my favourite male cousins. We hoped that our son would have cousin Dike's great virtues. We wanted good mentors and God-fearing people as his godparents. So we waited for the 11th of January 2008, but God had a different plan for us.

New Year's Eve 2007. Mike had gone to our home town, Ekwulobia, earlier that day to spend the New Year with his mother and the extended family. At midnight, my cousin Dike, his wife Yetunde and their toddler daughter Ure visited us at the hotel. They were on vacation from the United States. We all prayed for the safe delivery of our son who was to be born in the next few days.

My Tomorrow Shall Be Alright

I constantly wore two wristbands from the Redeemed Christian Church of God which my step-sister, Seun had sent to me after our summer vacation. The inscriptions on the wristbands were "My Tomorrow Shall Be Alright" and "Let Somebody Shout Halleluiah!"

The General Overseer of the Redeemed Christian Church of God (RCCG) Pastor Enoch Adeboye always began his sermon or would address his congregation with the phrase "Let Somebody Shout Hallelujah!" I wore those wristbands confessing and believing the words written on them.

Choosing The Baby Names

In the course of choosing names for our son, we had considered other names – "Nnanyelugo" which is Mike's traditional titled name and "Yobanna" which is the name of Mike's cousin who lives in Atlanta, Georgia. I thought of the popular acronym DKNY (Donna Karan New York) as cousin Dike was sometimes called. The name Yobanna however appealed to me and became engraved in my heart.

As we deliberated on the baby names, Mike suddenly decided our son would be called "Nadim". He said since the family business was called Nadim, he would rather choose Nadim as a second name for our son. He also said we would call our home and the properties within it Nadim Estate. In his excitement, he predicted and prophesied that Nadim would be a great name for our son. At this point, we left it to God to arrange the rest of the baby names after delivery.

Necrotizing Entereocolitis

Dike was born on the 7th of January 2008 at 11:14pm. It was not a difficult birth but we noticed that for 3 days our son had no reflex to suck. The doctors were worried and had no clue why this was because he appeared normal and was delivered without incident, despite being born two weeks before his expected delivery date (EDD); he was not a premature baby.

On the advice of the paediatrician, the nurses had taken to feeding Dike with glucose water using a syringe. He had refused to drink this, so we were advised to feed him with baby formula but he wouldn't eat this either. The nurses managed to force-fee him with only 10mls of the formula. His abdomen was a little firm, like that of a well fed baby, but not distended. Physiologically, there was nothing to indicate that the baby had any medical challenges.

On the morning of 9th January 2008, when the midwife came to give him a sponge bath, she observed that he had passed some abnormal stool. She showed it to me and expressed her concern due to its presentation. It had a reddish hue like mashed liver and had little whitish particles in it. She asked what I thought of it and I told her that I did not know. She took it to the senior midwife who immediately called the attention of the paediatrician who was alarmed and advised that all efforts to feed the baby be stopped.

The paediatricians had a quick consultation and afterwards set up an intravenous line to start him on some antibiotics. They informed me that this course of treatment would go on for some weeks until the ailment was cured, if he survived it at all.

The paediatrician later explained to me in more details what they suspected was wrong with Dike. I was horrified when she said they thought he had necrotizing enterocolitis which is a baby killer. Most babies who had it ended up with perforated intestines and required surgery; most would not survive the procedure. I wept.

They were still puzzled as to how Dike had survived after about thirty-six hours post-delivery with no visible symptoms of NEC as the ailment is usually called. Apparently, most babies that were delivered with NEC in our part of the world often died a few hours after delivery.

The paediatrician advised me to pray fervently for my baby to survive this ordeal given that he had come as a gift of joy to my family of three daughters. I then knew that we had to fight a battle to prevent possible grief to our family.

I have always believed in the use of pacifiers for babies, especially after having delivered two of my children in the United States where they always stick pacifiers into babies' mouths right from birth. The doctors and nurses had cautioned me several times against using pacifiers for Dike because as we were in the tropics, they believed the baby could ingest germs, particularly if the pacifier was not sterilized or if it kept falling out of his mouth. However, after the diagnosis, the paediatrician told me Dike would be hungry for the many days as he would not be allowed to eat. When I asked her if I should give him the pacifier, she said I would probably have a lot of stress especially from sleeplessness as a result of his cries from hunger therefore I should pacify him anyway I could.

Dike was hungry and it was an ordeal to behold as I watched the intravenous fluid drop once every few minutes. When I asked why it would not be made to flow faster, the paediatrician explained to me that it wasn't the regular intravenous fluid, but a cocktail of antibiotics that should be absorbed slowly or else it would cause more damage than good. I was also advised to keep visitors away to reduce the risk of infections to the baby.

While we nurtured Dike, the slow drops of the drip made the days drag. I committed Dike to the Lord and promised that if he were delivered from this affliction, I would present him back God and ensure he served Him all his life. I continued to thank God for his life for I had an inner conviction that it was useless dwelling on fear because whatever would be, would still be.

I told myself that if it was God's perfect will that the baby did not survive, then it will be God's way of saving me from the turbulent days and years that were to come. I reflected on a poem which I wrote in 1996 and it gave me an assurance of hope.

Peace

As I waited with arms opened wide
I prayed with my eyes lifted high
I felt the presence of the Lord very far
I thought He wouldn't hear my cry.
But I waited

I was in such a hurry
I grabbed the solutions I found
I heard the voice again and again
But then peace engulfed me
In a whisper all I heard was
Peace Peace Peace.
My peace I give unto you

His eyes were focused on me
And as I looked unto Him
With arms opened wide
I heard the sound in the silence
And peace engulfed me….
I thought I heard Him say
'My peace I give to you'.

Three days after Dike's birth, he developed jaundice and was put on phototherapy.

Serendipity

A few days after his birth, my friend Grace-Anne visited us in hospital and I briefed her on the challenge we were facing. She said she would tell our predicament to a Reverend Sister whom she regarded as her mother–in-the-Lord, and ask her to uphold us in prayers. She later got the Reverend Sister to speak with me. She told me she had already raised an altar to God on behalf of Dike and there was a battle raging. She advised me to pray, asking God to give Dike peace and save him. She further told me to say this prayer round the clock and encouraged me to have faith in spite of the battle at hand. I was emotional yet spiritually strengthened, for the Lord took away the spirit of fear within me and filled my heart with joy.

I reflected on the circumstances surrounding Dike's birth, his birthday and his names and saw that there was a pattern forming. As I became more prayerful, I had revelations from the Lord to start documenting as much as I could about the circumstances surrounding Dike's life.

Despite the pain from the caesarean section, the sleeplessness and the agony of watching Dike cry, I had peace within me. I was aware that the pattern of what I believed was unfolding, was not mere coincidence but orchestrated in God's perfect plan for our son's life.

On Dike's thirteenth day post-delivery, a visiting consultant from the teaching hospital examined him and certified him well. They had drawn some fluid from his stomach through his nostrils and after laboratory analysis, the consultant advised the discontinuation of the intravenous medication. I was asked to feed him and I did. Dike sucked with joy for his frail body needed his mother's milk. I was so relieved that the ordeal of starvation was over; I praised the Lord for delivering our son from premature death as a result of NEC.

Dike's bilirubin level had been low but a few days later it rose again. By the weekend, it had gone up a bit more and my hopes of being discharged dimmed. We had to wait for the tests on Monday for the decision to be discharged. Between Saturday and Monday morning, his blood level had gone up from 8.2 g/dl to 8.4 g/dl. His bilirubin level however, seemed abnormal but we were advised not to worry as it would likely normalize on its own within a few days. The paediatrician advised that we be discharged as soon as Dike's bilirubin level showed a significant decrease.

We were glad to be discharged and allowed to go home on Monday the 21st of January 2008, two weeks after Dike's birth. Our hopes were high and our hearts filled with joy for the victory over the battle with necrotizing enterocolitis which we believed was over. We went home with our little bundle of joy.

Dike was fair and very handsome with long smooth hair. Our little baby reminded us all of Mowgli, the little Indian boy who grew up with the animals in the movie, *The Jungle Book*. Dike had weighed 3kg at birth but at the time of his discharge fourteen days later, he was 2.6kg. We were told that it was alright for he would begin to add weight in no time.

The next day, I became worried as he did not tolerate the antibiotic syrup he was given on discharge. I called the paediatrician and she asked me to bring him back to the hospital for observation. This I did and his blood sample was taken. The result showed that his haemoglobin count was 8.6 g/dl and the paediatrician advised that the antibiotic be discontinued.

Dike continued to be administered the blood tonic but he passed stool as soon as he ate. We wondered if this was as a result of the blood tonic he was on, or simply the infancy season of frequent diaper changes, eating and sleeping. My aunt, Mummy Ida (my late mother's twin sister), had come for the *omugwo*, which is the Igbo custom where a mother visits to nurse and support her daughter who has just given birth. As a result of the frequent stooling, she called him "Li-Nyu"- a name that sounded Chinese but literally means "eat and poo" in the Igbo language.

We went for the next medical appointment on the 1st of February 2008. Dike looked so fair complexioned that the paediatrician took a puzzled look at him.

"Is this baby meant to be a white baby or what?" She asked as she took a curious look at him.

She then took him to the window and observed him in the daylight; she decided to do a blood count.

When the results came in, she told us that the haemoglobin count had dropped to 8.2 g/dl and wondered why the blood count was decreasing despite the blood tonic she had placed him on. She decided to do a blood transfusion immediately and I quickly called my husband who was at the airport on his way to Lagos for my younger brother's wedding. When I explained the situation to him, he rushed back to meet us at the hospital, donated the required blood then rushed off to board the evening flight to Lagos. As Mike left us, my Aunt and I took Dike home to prepare for a return to the hospital later that evening.

The blood transfusion began just before midnight and I stayed awake all night watching as the blood circulated round Dike's body. I was amazed as I watched his body go from all white to having patches of dark skin as the blood circulated through his system. It was unbelievable. The nurse checked his temperature and vital signs every 15 minutes during the transfusion to ensure all was well. The next morning, the paediatrician saw Dike and was pleased with his transformation.

"So this is a dark baby after all. Praise God!" She remarked.

After the observations, she discharged us and waived the hospital bill for the procedure, which was such a relief after the expenses we had incurred from Dike's birth and prolonged hospital admissions after the battle with NEC. Dike now had a healthier weight of 3.2kg from the 2.35kg he weighed prior to the blood transfusion.

We praised the Lord once more for His mercies and grace upon the life of our son.

The Gathering Storm

Mummy Ida stayed with us for the first two months of Dike's life. Dike continued to gain weight and by the 7th of March 2008, he weighed 3.85kg. It was Mummy Ida's birthday so we took her out for a celebratory dinner at the Protea Hotel. As my late mother's twin sister, she had often played the motherly role towards me and to my children who fondly called her grandma.

By the 19th of March 2008, Dike weighed 4.2kg and continued to grow into a handsome little baby boy. He had occasional stomach troubles and I hoped that it had nothing to do with the NEC which he had survived. The paediatricians assured me that it was probably just colic which a lot of infants experience. The days were good and filled with joy as we entertained the numerous guests who came to welcome our new bundle of joy. Grandma often put Dike on her chest while she lay down on the bed and he got very used to being carried that way.

As the days passed, we observed that Dike's eyes were light yellow. A few of our guests observed that too and suggested we treat him the old fashioned way of treating jaundice which was taking the baby out in the early morning sun to get some vitamin D. Grandma dutifully did this, but as the days and weeks passed, Dike's yellow eyes became more pronounced.

Ignorantly, I felt that Dike had already won a battle and this was the end of his ordeal. How totally mistaken and naïve I was.

We took Dike to the hospital several times to ask the paediatricians' opinion on his frequent stool and the cause of the yellowness of his eyes. Yet each time, we were assured that our son was normal and the yellowing of his eyes would eventually clear as the jaundice had been treated successfully. In the meantime, Dike was gaining weight, his stool was golden yellow and his vital signs seemed okay. I refused to worry but continued to lift Dike up in prayers to the Lord.

We observed that Dike's eyes would be clear on some days and on other days, would have a light tint of yellow. For the first two months as I recuperated, we ignorantly assumed that Dike was also recuperating from NEC. Unfortunately, the paediatricians did not advise for a liver function test to justify their belief that he was okay.

When Dike was barely two months old, I observed that his stool was very yellow and seemed to have a lot of oil in it. My aunt and I asked the paediatrician for her opinion but once again we were assured that the colour was normal. However, after a few weeks I observed that his stool had become lumpy and sometimes looked like beads and granules. I became worried but I was told that it was okay because the colour was golden yellow.

I remember that on one of those days, I observed that Dike's stool looked like beads of various sizes and I was so sure it was very abnormal. I could no longer believe these paediatricians whom I had depended on for their expertise concerning my son's health. I had believed in their professional judgment and I did not think I could argue with them on such issues. I was also dealing with my own pain from having had a caesarean section, the stress of managing a new baby, caring for my other children and also running a home. I was tired and under pressure so it was easy for us to stay in our comfort zone by believing the paediatricians who said the baby was okay, than distress ourselves further by searching for a medical solution to an ailment we were assured did not exist. We did not realise that a storm was raging within.

CHAPTER 2

Omega

In the cool evening the 27th of March 2008 when Dike was two months and twenty days old, I lay on my bed feeling totally at peace. Dike was by my side, the children were out at play and Mike had travelled out of town.

Dike's chest seemed congested although he did not have a cold or a running nose. He would cough occasionally, about three times a day, but I did not know how significant that was. I was occasionally bothered by the presentation of his stool which had remained very beady for the past week and comprised of different sizes of oily balls. I suddenly had a premonition to take Dike to see our family paediatrician, Dr. Ekeoku. It was an urgency I could not ignore as I needed his opinion as an experienced paediatrician. In my heart, I erroneously assumed that the doctor would brush off my fears as unnecessary; little did I know that God was leading me to seek the facts from a very experienced paediatrician.

As we sat in the hospital reception awaiting our turn, I thought about the state of the health care in our country and prayed in my heart for better conditions in our hospitals and the professionalism of the medical practitioners. Healthcare is such a delicate issue in our country and I knew improved health care services would go a long way to save lives.

I also believe we need common sense and intelligence in matters of healthcare to safeguard our families from the clutches of death. I have done this for many years with my family. Most people end up suffering greatly especially in this part of the world for not paying attention to symptoms when illnesses manifest. I have often advised people to be aware of the medication prescribed for them and their children. It is important to understand your body system and that of your children; know what your children are allergic to and what they can tolerate.

It was soon my turn to see Dr. Ekeoku. He took a look at Dike and said that he appeared pale and asked if I had any problems with him. He took Dike and laid him on the examination table for a closer look. He asked for the medical history which I explained in a nutshell. After the preliminary examination, he told me there was a totally different problem with Dike. He emphasized that it had nothing to do with the NEC Dike had just recovered from. My heart skipped a beat as I observed the doctor's facial expression and body language. He handed my son to me and I sat rigidly, not knowing what to expect.

He said Dike was highly anaemic as his eyes were very yellow and his skin was very pale. He shook his head in a way that seemed alarming and he sighed. He asked me what the paediatricians had done, and I said, "Nothing". This was obviously not good.

Dr. Ekeoku had more questions for me; he asked if the

paediatricians had done another liver function test after we were discharged and I replied that they had not. He then asked if we had done an abdominal scan and once again I replied that we had not. To all his questions, the responses were negative.

"Oh, God! These people should have known what to do!" he exclaimed as he sat and shook his head.

I was alarmed and asked what the problem was. He said he suspected there was an obstruction but he would not give me an explanation until he had run some tests. He said we need to do a scan very early the next day, but presently we could do a full blood count and liver function tests in his lab to help his investigation.

When I checked Dike's diapers, there was some stool in it. I showed this to the Doctor and it was even worse than the sample I has shown him earlier. He concluded that we had a crisis in our hands and was very upset that the doctors had told me that the yellowing in Dike's eyes would clear with time when they should have done a routine test to check his condition.

When I left Dr. Ekeoku's office, I was chest fallen. I reminisced on my earlier thoughts about the state of our healthcare delivery and felt justified with my feelings. It was simply not efficient. I would have been lying down on my bed till the uneventful occurred before my very eyes but for my observations. I left the hospital, took my baby home and once more, prayerfully handed his health over to the Lord.

The next day, Dike had his abdominal scan and we took the result back to the hospital. The test seemed fine except for his haemoglobin which had dropped to an alarming 7.2 count despite the fact that he had had a blood transfusion about seven weeks earlier. His blood count was much lower than before he was transfused.

Dr. Ekeoku told me that irrespective of what was causing the blockage in his system, Dike needed a blood transfusion right away. I told him we would need to wait a few days as my husband was away in Abuja with our first daughter Ugonna, whom he had taken for the pre-admissions interview into the Nigerian Turkish International College. I called Mike immediately to update him on Dike's condition. He returned that weekend and on Monday, our second daughter Amaka and I spent the night at the hospital with Dike as he was transfused.

Dr. Ekeoku was still not satisfied with the test results. He gave us a note for the Managing Director of Pix Centre, asking him to do the scan himself as he was a more experienced radiologist. The report came back the same and I thought that was a reason to rejoice as it did not show any blockage. When Dr. Ekeoku read the report he was baffled because Dike's liver function test showed something was wrong yet the scan did not indicate anything was amiss.

The doctor still had his fears and told me clearly that every doctor knows his limits. He said he suspected hepatitis amongst other liver diseases in Dike's body and he told me my baby also had a respiratory tract infection. The doctor also considered the possibility of an allergy to breast milk so he prescribed NAN which is lactose free milk. He advised me to keep Dike off breast milk for about two weeks. I wondered if the NEC Dike had been treated for at birth had anything to do with his present condition.

Dike was treated for malaria and given intravenous antibiotic injections for five days. His breathing improved. Despite the hot and humid weather we did not use air-conditioning, resorting to using a fan occasionally. The blood transfusion made a great difference to his physiology; he smiled a lot and had greater energy. I was glad and very grateful to God that I made the decision to take him to Dr. Ekeoku. Dike was now three months old.

On the 3rd of April 2008, Dike had his first public outing. The children and I went to the University of Port-Harcourt for my Aunt's Professor Stella Ibe's inaugural lecture. She had just been made a professor and it was a grand occasion with some of her siblings in attendance. My maternal uncle Agunze was overwhelmed by Dike's handsomeness.

"This baby is so handsome!" he exclaimed. He was worried when he noticed the yellowness of Dike's eyes and I told him that Dike's condition was still under investigation. He advised that if we did not have very experienced doctors in Port-Harcourt, we should come to Lagos for further investigations and possible treatment.

At the reception after the event, my first daughter Ugonna was awed by the procession of the professors to the high table. She felt privileged as she was invited by her grand aunt to join in the procession. She whispered to my Aunt, "Grandma I am going to be a professor like you someday".

When the celebrations were over, we took Dike back to the hospital for his injection, a review of the tests and the second scan. We were advised to continue all medications and return for a check-up in a month's time.

The Battle

Monday the 14th of April 2008. I took Dike to see Dr. Ekeoku, arriving as he was seeing his last patient for the day. I wanted him to give us a referral to see the paediatric surgeon at the teaching hospital but he decided to call the surgeon to come to his office for the consultation instead. I was quite delighted with this because the consultant came within the hour which saved us the long trip to the teaching hospital, and the attending protocol of a general hospital.

Whilst waiting, I met Mrs. Ekeoku whom I had seen several

times but never had the opportunity to speak with. She told me that her husband had been praying for Dike and I was touched by her humility and their practical Christian life which had endeared many of their patients to them. Dr. Ekeoku always began and ended the day at the clinic with prayers with all his staff and any patients that were available to pray. He would often pray for his patients while consulting if the situation was one that seemed challenging. There were a few times I witnessed him anoint his patients with olive oil when in very grave situations and he had also done this with my children on several occasions.

Meanwhile, Dr. Ekeoku and the paediatric surgeon Dr. Gbobo, were in discussion. Afterwards, the surgeon explained to me the situation with Dike. He drew a sketch of the liver with the gall bladder and the stomach, and explained the biliary system. He said there is a narrow passage called the bile duct which connects the liver to the stomach, and despite its being extremely narrow, there was a total or partial obstruction which was causing the prolonged jaundice in Dike. This condition was called biliary atresia and from the scan reports which he reviewed, although there was not yet any evidence of damage to the liver, the liver function tests indicated a high alkaline phosphate of 172 IU/L.

He concluded that it was probably a case of biliary atresia with a partial obstruction which made Dike's stool gradually become clayey as he lacked the required amount of bilirubin to digest his food intake. This was hard to take in. I had seen Dike's stool change from one colour to another in the past one month. Sometimes the stool had a lot of oil floating in it, sometimes it was clayey, other times greenish, or with a mustard yellow hue, and some other times it was beady. I was very confused.

Again, I showed the surgeon the stool sample I had brought

with me and he confirmed it was a case of biliary atresia. He asked us to pray that the blockage would open up, even though he had never really seen this situation get better. He said an intervention surgery called a Kasai procedure was useful in correcting this anomaly and that the Japanese had more expertise in performing it. I left the hospital with a heavy heart and prayed all the way home, interceding with Dike's name Yobanna which means 'a plea to God for mercy'.

I went back to the hospital on Thursday for another consultation with the surgeon. I was asked to continue with the lactose free milk, reintroduce the breast milk and then come back in two weeks for another liver function test (LFT). We were to do a few more of these tests as the weeks progressed to get a clearer picture of the problem.

Once again, I handed Dike over to God while I made a conscious effort not to worry as I was becoming very anxious. I reminded myself that worrying would only yield negative results so I chose to praise God and plead continuously on Dike's behalf. I begged God to heal him and strengthen him, to give him peace and save him just as the Rev. Sister had earlier advised when she interceded for Dike at the time of his birth.

On the 18th of April 2008, I went back to the hospital for Dike's routine vaccinations. I went in to see the chief paediatrician at the hospital where Dike was born to brief her on Dike's situation and she was shocked about his condition. Amazingly, Dike remained strong and handsome, appearing healthy except for the colouration of his eyes. I told her that Dike's great physical appearance was as a result of God's favour towards us despite the challenge at hand. I believed that if God saw us through the battle with NEC, then He would also see us through biliary atresia.

Later that month, Dike's eyes seemed to have become lighter in colouration. However, I was amazed when someone asked me why Dike's eyes were greenish. I had observed earlier that day that the eyes were greenish but I convinced myself that it was a visual illusion. I quickly took Dike back to the hospital and the doctor confirmed that Dike's eye colouration had indeed become darker. He said Dike had been better the last time he saw us; he advised we see the paediatric surgeon for further consultation insisting we ask the surgeon to give us a referral letter to enable us take Dike out of the country for further treatment because his condition was beyond anyone's scope of treatment within Nigeria. He also asked me to enquire from the surgeon how long we might have to wait before we found a solution and how long it would take to prepare for the trip out of Nigeria.

As we prepared for our trip, we also faced the challenge of shortage in the supply of lactose free milk in the market; even a search in the Lagos markets yielded no results. Dr Ekeoku advised me to continue with the breast milk which I gladly did for it was a better option and was freely available. Occasionally Dike would vomit the breast milk and I became very worried the day he vomited so violently whilst we visited my aunt May. I committed Dike into God's hands as I was totally clueless on what to do next. I calmed my nerves by chanting "It is well" over and over again.

The Dedication

As we made plans to take Dike abroad for medical treatment, we also deemed it necessary for him to be baptised as we needed to present him to God. Dike was baptised on Saturday the 10th of May 2008 at our local church, Christ Church, Old GRA Port Harcourt, in the presence of family and a few close friends. My close friend Chika Peterside, who was a pillar of strength and support for me throughout Dike's pregnancy, was made his godmother. Dike's godfathers are my cousin Dike and Professor Felix Ideriah, an elder in our church and Mike's fellow Rotarian from the Rotary District 9140 in Port-Harcourt.

Dike's baptism was followed by a thanksgiving service and thereafter a photo session which we documented in Dike's special albums. We had a small reception; it was a brief but lovely celebration. For Mike and I, we were glad we had done the needful. We still had a major tussle to face and were anxious about the days ahead.

Ignorance And Guilt

We had an appointment with the paediatric surgeon, Dr. Gbobo, for Sunday the 4th of May 2008 at one of the clinics in Port Harcourt where he consulted. We discussed at length and he asked us to come to the university teaching hospital on Wednesday the 7th of May 2008, which was his clinic day, to collect a medical report for the referral overseas.

Dike now weighed 5.5kg, and was just three days short of his fourth month of life. I called my mother's younger sister, Dr. Nwosu who was then the Medical Director of the Federal Medical Hospital Lagos, to brief her on the paediatric surgeon's diagnosis. She asked that we send the medical report to her as soon as possible to forward to Apollo Hospital in Chennai, India.

Mike immediately contacted the hospital through their website and was surprised at their prompt response. We were delighted at the professionalism they exhibited in handling our enquiries.

Mike also needed a medical solution for his own health issues which resulted from gunshot wounds he had sustained during an attack by armed robbers in 1997. He had spent two months in hospital in Nigeria and subsequently we went for recuperation in the United States. His left arm still had a lot of pellets and he had remained in pain after several surgeries. He required further surgery to take out as many pellets as possible and to fix his arm muscles to enable him regain use of the arm as it had become stiff.

The medical team at Apollo Hospital asked for a recent x-ray of Mike's elbow and for Dike's medical report. They said they could deal with Mike's arm however, regarding Dike, we were informed that infants with biliary atresia were usually given the Kasai procedure at the age of two months or less for best results.

On hearing this news, I felt very bitter. I felt I had procrastinated about taking Dike for a second opinion. I felt guilty that we had repeatedly consulted at the hospital where Dike was born, but were repeatedly told not to worry about Dike's health despite all the evidence in his eyes and his stool, which indicated something was definitely wrong. Although my aunt Ida had questioned the paediatrician's judgment, we did not seek a second opinion but rather resolved to wait to see if the stain will resolve itself and also to allow him heal from the trauma of the treatment from NEC.

How wrong I was.

It was during this period that Mike's cousin, Mercy Ezeanya called. I had spoken to her a few times while in hospital after Dike's delivery and again after the discharge. This time she asked for Dike's names and when I told her, she said she had a name for him. She named him "Victory" and I acknowledged her pronouncement on our son and agreed to pass this information to Mike. Diken'agha literally means victor/victory. I asked myself if everything about Dike was merely coincidental or ordained.

The more I had these revelations, the more equipped I became for the challenge ahead, something I could not really comprehend at that time. The only thing I knew was that God had a special purpose and plan for this child, and He had given me peace despite the challenges we faced. I had been writing a journal and knew I had to keep writing through these challenges, so that there would be a record of how God would show His manifestation as King and the author of all things. It was also meant to build the faith of those who doubt God's ability to make all things perfect in His time. I knew it was vital that I had documented evidence of things that were and those that were yet to manifest.

During one of our consultations with the paediatric surgeon Dr. Gbobo, Mike expressed his concern about my anxiety for Dike, for he felt I worried too much. The doctor understood his concern and responded that I had every cause to worry especially as he had earlier emphasized that the medical intervention for this ailment was usually poor in this part of the world. Moreover, the Kasai procedure had only a twenty percent chance of success when done early enough, even in the developed world.

We asked Dr. Gbobo to write a referral letter to enable us take Dike overseas for treatment and he was delighted to know we could afford to. He asked me to see him at his office to collect the referral letter and a medical report during the week. As we left the doctor's clinic, I noticed that Dike had not passed much urine and the little stain I saw on his diaper was deep yellow. I was bothered by this so I gave him a lot of water to drink and fed him with breast milk.

The next day, I took Dike back to the hospital for blood tests. While I waited at the laboratory, I seized the opportunity to look at some specimens under a microscope. The laboratory technologist explained what I was looking at which gave me better insight into Dike's condition. In fact, it further opened my eyes to a lot of things about the human body. I was anxious to know more about the liver function tests (LFT) so he showed me how the concentrated blood is spun to separate the samples used for the test. He explained that if one were jaundiced, the part separated would be stained. Seeing how yellow Dike's extracted sample was, I then understood that hoping the colour in the eyes would clear was simply wishful thinking for with the lecture I had received from the paediatric surgeon a day earlier, I finally understood a lot more about the liver and the biliary system and the challenge we faced. I began to pray for a miracle of healing.

Worries

I tried hard to be brave and worry less although sometimes, the unpredictability of the whole situation overwhelmed me. Once again, I began to feel guilty for procrastinating after our discharge from the hospital. It began to bother me more when I noticed that Dike had not passed urine for two days after we saw Dr. Gbobo. This new development worried me very much.

I went to the University of Port-Harcourt Teaching Hospital for Dike's scan and I ran into my aunt, Professor Ibe. I told her what I had observed and she said children are occasionally saved from serious ailments when they have intelligent mothers who have chosen to be informed on the facts about their children's conditions. She affirmed that everything I had noticed about Dike was brought to the attention of the doctors because I am not an ignorant mother. This had probably saved his life.

There was a long waiting list at the Radiology Department of UPTH but we were lucky to have the intervention of Professor Akanni, an obstetrician and gynaecologist who is an uncle to my cousin Rumundaka. He insisted the radiologist's attendants lead us in to see the radiologist. We went in and the radiologist spent time searching for the gall bladder as he scanned Dike but he could only see the liver and the kidneys. He asked when the baby was fed and I told him at 9am, two hours earlier. I had deliberately kept Dike fasting for two hours since he had eaten just in bits on the days we did the two scans at Pix Center. The radiologist's report at Pix Center showed that the liver was dilated, therefore the gall bladder would not be seen.

Keeping Dike fasting, however, did not make any difference since the radiologist did not see the gall bladder. The team analysed their findings and said the liver was about 9cm but ought to be about 6cm for his age. With the report I had a cause to weep.

Earlier on in the day, I had made a dental appointment with Dr. Tayo Fashakin, at the teaching hospital dental section. I took Dike with me to see Dr. Fashakin and he met me in a weepy mood. He encouraged me to go ahead and fix my teeth, to ensure I got at least one problem solved that day. I did and was glad that I was able to fill two cavities and another two I did not know had existed in my dentition. I left the teaching hospital afterwards and went to the hospital where Dike's was born to get his medical report.

I arrived at the hospital in a very sober mood and I became upset when the receptionist rudely informed me I had to pay a consultation fee before seeing the paediatrician. I insisted I did not need to consult with any doctor but to simply ask for my son's medical report. She said I should see a general practitioner and I was enraged because the hospital management knew that my son had a medical challenge yet did not call to follow up on his progress. I had only come for a medical report and I was being asked to pay for consultation which I did not think was fair to me. I told the attendant that the paediatrician wanted to see me so I walked out on her and went straight into the paediatric unit while I struggled to curtail my burning anger.

When the attending paediatricians saw that I came into her office without Dike, she panicked and began to ask questions about his health. I assured her that he was alive and sleeping in the car where I had left him with his nanny and my driver. When she and the attending nurse in the paediatric unit questioned me about Dike's condition, I became emotional and finally broke down in tears. The Chief Paediatrician came into the office at that moment and was surprised to see me in tears. She took me into her office and I told her I had come to get a medical report to enable us make travel plans for Dike's treatment abroad. I also informed her that my immediate concern was Dike's infrequent flow of urine in the past three days. She said she hoped he had not developed what was called valves which she explained were blockages in the urethra that could be solved by a medical procedure. The procedure could only be done effectively at Saint Nicholas Hospital Lagos, but she advised that a scan should be done first to determine the condition of the urethra. She asked me to watch out for a normal flow of urine while bathing him. A normal urine she said, flows like a fountain but if the urine came out in droplets then one might have a cause to worry.

She pacified me and assured me that a urinary tract problem would usually take a while before it affects the kidneys. She then wrote the report and I left in time to pick my daughters from school.

I was scheduled to see Dr. Ekeoku that evening after I picked up the lab result from his hospital. Surprisingly, Dike's alkaline phosphates had significantly dropped in comparison to the results of the two previous tests. The first was 214 IU/L and the second was 232 IU/L. The current one from UPTH was 147IU/L while the one from Omega Hospital was 111.2IU/L.

Dr. Ekeoku did an edema check on Dike and said there was no need to worry but advised me to give him a lot of water to drink and if he did not pass normal urine by the next day, I should bring him back. He also suggested I weigh Dike daily to rule out water retention in his body.

I felt guilt once more as I realised I had not given him a lot of water since he was now taking a lot of medication which included blood tonic, vitamins, folic acid, cough syrup and Allergin, in addition to formula and the breast milk. I gave Dike a lot of water to drink and was overjoyed when I bathed him the next day as I watched him pass normal urine, though little in quantity. I was grateful to God that Dike eventually passed a normal stream of urine but I wondered if the challenge was caused by my introducing formula to him two weeks earlier without increasing his water intake. I acknowledged that experience is the best teacher as I recalled that my mother-in-law had asked me for the baby's water every now and then. I would give her the water to feed him but never really took note of the quantity he took. I eventually got a better understanding on how water helps flush out impurities and dilute the concentration of urea in the body.

As this challenge was resolved I recalled the Bible verse, Matthew 6:34 "Sufficient unto the day is the evil thereof."

On Wednesday, I went early to University of Port Harcourt Teaching Hospital to collect the medical report from Doctor Gbobo. It was a long wait and once again, I ran into Dr. Akanni and we discussed Dike's condition. He said he would seek advice from his wife who is a paediatrician and get back to me.

As I went back to wait in the reception, a friend Dr. Amaka Okorie, came by to see me. Our mutual friend, Dr. Bassey Fiebai had informed her that I was there to see the paediatric surgeon. She said she would help me search the internet for hospitals in Japan as Dr. Akanni had suggested for they both acknowledged that India would be cheaper but might be saddled with third world factors. We wanted the best solution to Dike's ailment but also at an affordable cost. Amaka insisted we acted as quickly as possible because she had also been through a medical challenge with her son and she understood the effect of timely interventions.

We finally saw Dr. Gbobo and he wrote the report I came for. He asked a young intern to take me to the typist in another part of the hospital. The very clumsy young doctor kept me waiting for almost thirty minutes while sipping a bottle of coca cola despite my urging him to do the needful. He eventually took me to the typist who was busy chatting with her colleagues and refused to acknowledge my presence. I had to wait for forty minutes as the typist insisted on having her lunch while she gossiped with her colleagues. At some point, I had to stand in front of her with Dike in my arms, to remind her that I was waiting for the letter on the instruction of the paediatric surgeon who was waiting for me to come back to him with the letter. She rudely told me to sit down so she would not choke on her food. Having spent half of the day to get the medical report, it was annoying having to wait longer for it to be typed. I was upset but my better judgment made me control my emotions. I only prayed our paths would not have to cross any time in the near or distant future. The lackadaisical attitude to public work and the lack of respect for authority is so deplorable and a shame.

After all the delays, I prayed that I would get the letter processed and stamped by the hospital administrator so I would not have to come back the following day to collect it. It eventually took about two hours to get the editing done and then stamped before we went home.

I left the hospital with Dike's medical report feeling extremely disenchanted with our people's attitude to work. I was grateful to

God that I had in my possession, the document I needed. I handed my son's case to God, affirming that if the Lord had brought us that far, He would not forsake us, but will give us the grace to forge on to victory.

The Dream: My Tomorrows Shall Be All Right

I dream very often and as a creative person, most of my works are revealed to me in my day or night dreams usually before dawn. I usually see the circumstances I am experiencing which is a rare gift I became aware of in my youth. I also learnt to ask God questions about those issues that baffle me when I get those dreams. I would often receive an immediate answer and a confirmation later in the day through various other means such as in a passage of the Bible, a book, a signpost, a sermon or through some random persons.

In the midst of our challenge, it suddenly occurred to me that I had not yet dreamt about Dike. That same night I specifically asked the Lord for a revelation concerning Dike's situation and as I slept I found myself in a classroom where we did some landscape paintings. In that dream, each student had to be tested. Everyone had to tear off a page in a calendar and reproduce whatever picture one got. I saw Nkeiru Ndefo, my classmate from secondary school whom I had not seen in over twenty four years. She had painted a view from the top of a hill overlooking the beach. There were some high rise buildings across the road and the sea on another side. The surroundings in her painting was covered in thick mud from a landslide and some areas were covered by lava as a result of a volcanic eruption.

I looked at the picture, trying to analyse the concept of this artwork which failed to make much sense to me except for the disaster it depicted. I soon began to decipher the unseen images and tried to explain my views to the others in the classroom. This mental image took me back to my literature class in secondary school, where I seemed to understand the unseen prose more than the other students who found the subject Literature-in-English very boring. In those days, some of my classmates would often ask me to explain the day's lecture to them after class. I had realised then in secondary school that I was gifted to teach and the more I taught, the clearer and more interesting the subjects became to me.

In the dream, the class instructor asked some of us to board a glider that would fly over the area to enable us get a clearer view of the landscape for the project at hand. This was done in batches and was a routine experience in that special art class. My first daughter Ugonna and two other persons were in my batch. Four of us sat at the outermost passenger section of the glider with one foot each hanging down the craft, as it was loaded to capacity. I asked that we all hold hands so none of us would fall out. As we gently glided, my shoes loosened and I bent forward to adjust it so it would not fall into the sea below.

As we glided over the hilltop and all over the landscape which I had seen earlier from the calendar, we made a turn to land at the point where we had started the glide. Suddenly, as I made to catch one of my shoes which again was about to fall off, a male paratrooper jumped out of the glider, landed on his legs and held onto the glider, helping us land gently as though from a parachute. We were all excited and hung there to watch another flight which was an acrobatic demonstration by a group of paratroopers.

After a while, having watched some parts of the show, most of the students went back into the class room, leaving just a few of us outside. As the air show went on, those of us outside talked about the expedition. One of the gliders was operated by a captain and his assistant called Peter. They gently landed upright near us and suddenly were transformed into tiny creatures trapped in a vessel in the shape of a champagne bottle. A feeling of panic overwhelmed us as we watched the two creatures and we instinctively ran to pull them out of the vessel. One among us tried to dissuade the rest of us from rescuing them and was of the opinion that what we were watching was part of the show. He said the Captain and Peter were experienced paratroopers and would be able to let themselves out of the vessel. On hearing this, everyone ignored the distressed two and carried on with their idle talks. I was not convinced by the guy's explanation for I clearly saw the expression of distress on the two men and as I pondered on how to help rescue them, we suddenly heard a loud pop. We looked at the vessel and saw foam come out of the nozzle of the champagne bottle. It dawned on us all that the men had actually been trapped and in danger of asphyxiation. We rushed to them but we could not get them out as there was too much pressure in the bottle which continued to expel white foam.

As we tried in the rescue mission to no avail, a young beggar who hung around the neighbourhood came by and suggested we put the bottle under a tap to flush out the contents. It seemed like a brilliant idea but as we tried this, the beggar quickly fastened the nozzle of the bottle to the tap. I became more alarmed as I saw a greater danger in what he did. I pushed the young man out of the way and unplugged the bottle from the tap thereby allowing Peter and the captain pop out instead of drowning. They came out, coughing and choking but within a short while, they quickly recovered and were on their feet.

This beggarly young man who had tried to help immediately produced what seemed like an SOS note which had popped out of the bottle much earlier. It showed that the duo had been trapped since the beginning of the flight, in the early hours of the day. Unfortunately, there had been no way the note could reach us as we had been busy discussing and had not paid them any attention to understand they were in distress.

I woke up from my sleep and it was easy to relate the dream to Dike's condition after all I had asked for a special revelation from God. I related the scenario of the landslide and the volcanic eruption, our flight, and the bewilderment of the trapped paratroopers to our reality. My watchword had been "delay is dangerous". I knew also that ignorance was even worse than delay. The dream was a clear revelation of Dike's struggle with necrotising enterocolitis and biliary atresia, but I wondered if the end of the dream was the future outcome of his ailment.

I was assured through the revelation that the manifestations were at the appointed time and that we would probably reach a point where only the grace of God would normalize the situation that seemed impossible with man. With the revelation, I became mentally armed and ready for the battle. I did not know which route it would take, I just made up my mind to put my hope and trust in God with unflinching faith, knowing that the battle, the victory and the glory belonged to God.

I had peace of mind as I continuously prayed with the few family members and friends who believed and stood in faith with us.

Fear Factor

We had made up our minds to take Dike to India, and on the 15th of May 2008, we set out for our trip to Chennai in South India.

Chika, my bosom friend came by to see her godson Dike, and to pray with us before our departure from home. Our daughters had gone to school and were to stay with Chika and her family all through the duration of our trip to India. Chika held Dike and began to sob as we stood in my dining room. I tried to pacify her, but instead

I found myself crying with her. We said a prayer of agreement for God to save Dike before we said our goodbyes. We went through Mike's office on our way to the airport and I took pictures of Mike as he carried Dike. As we drove to the airport, I was low in spirit as different thoughts came to my mind which centred on Dike's chances of survival. I wondered if he would come back to Nigeria a healthy child and if he will take pictures with his father in that office again. I rebuked the thought. Then again I recalled that Dike was born looking like a little Indian boy.

"What if he is truly going to India where he belongs and does not come back?"

As these thoughts came to my mind, I pushed them out as I silently prayed.

I sent text messages to the paediatric surgeon Dr. Gbobo and to Dr. Ekeoku, and they both called me to wish us well. I became emotional and I had a lump in my throat. We bought our tickets from Aero-Contractors and were the last to board the aircraft. As we walked on the embankment into the airplane, I saw my close friend Fama Graham Douglas, who was also boarding another flight; she was shocked to see Dike with his eyes so jaundiced.

Tears immediately welled up in her eyes for she did not realise what we had gone through since the birth of the son she had rejoiced over. As we talked, we saw some school children on an excursion to the airport. Once more, I wondered if Dike would be back and if he would ever grow up to be a normal school child like them. I became very emotional as Fama and I parted. I walked into the cabin and I saw Chief Obiyo, our third daughter Dalu's godfather. We exchanged pleasantries despite my emotional state and he cheered me up as I proceeded to my seat. Mike also called to cheer me up as we sat down to prepare for take-off. I braced up and told myself that death will not get a hold of the baby God had given us for our joy to be complete. I asked myself why I was grieving the Holy Spirit by mourning a happy baby who looked healthy, instead of praising the Lord as he said we should in every situation.

In Lagos, I stayed with my uncle Agunze and my aunt Asadiche in their Ikoyi home and on Sunday, Dike and I went to church with Tonye; later we attended house fellowship with him. His fellowship members had prayed for me at a time I was asking God's direction on where to go for Dike's delivery. They had also been praying for us during our challenge with NEC. It was my pleasure to attend fellowship with them and present the baby they had prayed for.

During the fellowship, I shared Dike's testimony and we all claimed victory over the enemy. We prophesied that he would grow up to love God and work in His vineyard; that he would lead a great number of men and women to the Lord; that he would be a blessing to his parents, siblings, family, school, his peers, his church, his state, his country Nigeria, the Indians and to the entire world and that he will not be cut short in his prime but will bury his parents in his old age.

I decreed that Dike will amaze the doctors because the Bible says in Matthew 19:26 that with God all things are possible, for God's report supersedes the doctor's report. After they made the proclamation of blessings over us, we left feeling very enabled for our journey.

Delays

I had planned that we would travel on the 19th of May 2008, but were told we needed some medical documentation from Emirates Airlines on the advice of our travel agent. At the office, I was asked to fill a medical form, send to our doctor for endorsement, scan the form to the Emirates e-mail address then wait for three working days for a response. We could travel on the next available flight if we were cleared to travel. This information surprised and bothered me because my travel agent had only said I just needed to go to Emirate office and fill a form before we could travel.

I called the travel agent to reschedule the flight for Thursday, which was the day Mike had been scheduled to meet with us in Chennai.

I went to my Aunt Dr. Nwosu's office at the Federal Medical Centre situated at the Railway Compound, formerly the Nigerian Railways Hospital, in Ebute Metta Lagos to get the documents signed. Afterwards, I went to my brother's office to scan the documents and send to the Emirates office as required. This done, I went back to my uncle's home to wait a few more days; it turned into a ten-day ordeal.

Interestingly, the Open Heavens devotional for Friday the 23rd of May 2008 had the headline 'Man can delay your situation, but they cannot stop the plan God has for you'.

I had been frustrated by an Emirates staff who led me to believe he was doing me a favour by giving me his cell phone number, which he did not normally give out to customers. He said I could not reach him during the office hours because he would not answer telephone calls as he was usually overworked. He said he would call me once he had a positive word for me. The days dragged, as I patiently awaited his call which never came.

On Wednesday, I called the Emirates Airlines staff and was told that their computers were down; he told me he was going to the airport to work and that we would most likely travel on Saturday. I called again on Thursday for a confirmation for Saturday and he said it would be on Monday. This upset me greatly. At that point, my uncle who was by me on the dinner table grabbed the phone from my hands. He raged at the man for his lousy manner in handling an affair that ought to have been an emergency.

My uncle had, in the past one week, travelled thrice to the eastern, western and northern states of Nigeria. Each time he returned home, he met me without a confirmation of a travel date. I was so infuriated that I developed a migraine and was glad Dike slept all through the night, so I was also able to get some sleep as well.

On Thursday morning, I decided to seize the opportunity of the delay to apply for the USA non-immigrant visa for my family; only our first and third daughters were USA citizens by birth. I was lucky to find only two open dates for the appointments in July, hoping that we would be back from India by then. I called the Emirates staff again and was told he would have a word for me by Saturday. He then advised that I buy an infant oxygen mask, which is a requirement for a baby that requires medical attention, though the airline would provide the oxygen if the need arose. My uncle and aunt took me to buy the oxygen mask which was never used and still remains in my closet.

Effects Of A Report

On 24th of May 2008 at The Redeemed Christian Church of God house fellowship centre, we discussed the topic of faith. I was of the opinion that you either had faith or you did not because there were times when one lacked faith in particular situations. In Dike's situation for instance, I had faith that the result would be good. After I spoke, Tonye explained that everyone had faith, no matter how little, because Jesus said "ye men of little faith" which simply justifies that fact. I agreed with him and I asked, "Like having faith as little as the mustard seed?" He affirmed that I got the point. We also discussed understanding revelations from God's Word and also receiving confirmation from people or through whatever means the Lord chooses to confirm a revelation to us. I immediately told God once more to show me within a week another revelation to hold unto.

The following day, I went with my aunt Joy to see her cousin and I saw a copy of the Open Heavens daily devotional written by the General Overseer of The Redeemed Christian Church of God, Pastor E.A. Adeboye. I immediately knew I needed this heavenly tool for my earthly mission and challenge. I quickly called Tonye to ask if he could get me a copy but our hostess Mrs. Ifunanya Udoji, told me she had a spare copy which she could give me. I was glad as I spent a few hours reading the text for the previous day titled "Effects of a Report". The Bible reference was Joshua 14: 8:

> "Nevertheless, my brethren who went up with me made the heart of the people melt, but I wholly followed the Lord my God."
> Joshua 14: 8

The narrative also stated that Numbers 13:27-33 tells us certain things about a report.

Your assessment of a situation influences its outcome. Numbers 13: 30-32:

> "And Caleb stilled the people before Moses, and said, Let us go up at once, and possess it; for we are well able to overcome it. But the men that went up with him said, we be not able to go up against the people; for they are stronger than we. And they brought up an evil report of the land which they had searched unto the children of

> Israel, saying, the land, through which we have gone to search it, is a land that eateth up the inhabitants thereof; and all the people that we saw in it are men of a great stature."
> Numbers 13: 30-32

> Indeed, the ailments Dike had were those that devoured the afflicted, however like Caleb's report, I stood in faith that the devil would not make minced meat out of my son. I had confessed and prophesied that fact a day earlier at the house fellowship, therefore I chose to stand on God's Word and His report which is life and not death. "I was forty year old when Moses the servant of the Lord sent me from Kadesh Barnea to spy out the land and I brought back word to him as it was in my heart."
> Joshua 14:7

Having read the above Bible passage in the Open Heavens I personalized it thus: "I, Chinwe was forty years old when my children's paediatrician advised me to go abroad to find a medical solution for my ailing son Diken'agha. He prayed over us and told us that every doctor has his limit, but God is the unlimited doctor. He had seen miracles happen in hopeless situations; therefore he said we should go with the Lord and never ever give up. God had directed us to India and I knew I would bring back the word to him as it was in my heart."

I proclaimed once more that Diken'agha Kenechukwu Nadim Yobanna Victory Ezeanya would not die but would live to declare the works of the Lord. I affirmed that Diken'agha is no grass hopper; Dike by name is a mighty warrior in battle. By connotation he is victorious, and thankful to God for making him who he is. He is penitent and obedient in prayer.

Pastor Adeboye holds the view that in life, your views must be handled with caution to enable you achieve your expected result. The first lesson here is that your report or response to life's challenges determines the degree to which you follow God. Your report will show whether you follow Him fully, closely or from a distance like Peter did in Mark 14: 54:

> "And Peter followed him afar off, even into the palace of the high priest: and he sat with the servants, and warmed himself at the fire."
> Mark 14: 54

Your action and reaction will also show if you are not following Him at all. What does your report speak concerning you? Accepting an evil report, which is a report below God's words, means you have stopped following Him.

> "The light of the eyes rejoiceth the heart: and a good report maketh the bones fat."
> Proverbs 15:30

A report either adds or subtracts; it either weakens or fortifies the hearer. Are you an evil reporter, pulling down what God is building? Any statement that cannot add something positive to someone's life is a bad report.

Another lesson is that the quality of a report is determined by what fills the heart of the reporter. In Joshua 14:7, Caleb said his report came from his heart since his report was filled with faith, when the hopeless situation concerning the promise was fed into it, the end result was hope.

I took time to note everything on the first day I read the devotional. I believed it was the confirmation of what was discussed in the House Fellowship a few days earlier. I was truly grateful for the word of God that came to me; it was the confirmation I had once more specifically asked of which I needed to show me God had an upper hand in our affairs. No matter the challenge, He would make us victorious if we had faith even if it was as little as the mustard seed.

This revelation also taught me, as Pastor Adeboye holds, that we do not have to wait until the unexpected happens before we look frantically for solutions from God's words, rather, we should feed our hearts steadily with scripture. As long as our hearts are right, this will definitely affect our end results.

> "Keep thy heart with all diligence for out of it are the issues of life."
> Proverbs 4:23

Reports emanate from the heart and it is the state of your heart that gives shape and meaning to developments around you.

> "Ye are of God, little children and have overcome them: because greater is He that is in you than he that is in the world."
> 1 John 4:4

Pastor Adeboye advised that if situations and circumstances still embarrass you, it is because the presence of Jesus in your life is too insignificant to overcome the forces outside. For Jesus to grow in your heart, you need to soak yourself in God's Word regularly, studying, memorizing and meditating on it. If you want your heart to continue to dictate the outcome of situations you experience, then stick with God's Word. Draw closer to Jesus and be filled with His Spirit.

I sent Tonye a text message stating:

> "As I meditated on God's words this morning, I saw clearly a confirmation of what we believe and expect in the Open Heavens titled 'Effect of a Report'."

I had sent a text message to Dr. Ekeoku earlier informing him of our delay in Lagos to which he sent a touching reply.

"Just saw your text now, never mind, all things work together for good to them that love God. This delay could turn out to be Dike's deliverance. Be rest assured that we are praying for Dike. God blesses you. Dr. Ekeoku."

I can only say that this text message warmed my heart. We were in Lagos delayed by Emirates Airlines, yet rather than remain frustrated, I seized the opportunity to socialize and dwell on the worthy. I studied the Bible, I wrote my journal, and I had been able to get a US Embassy interview date with the hope that we would be back from India in time for the scheduled appointment. I gave God all the glory as I went back to bed around 5am that Saturday morning. I woke up with two dreams and immediately sat up to write about them in my journal.

In the first dream, I saw a woman holding her son and walking along a busy street. I felt there was a spiritual problem with the little boy who kept scratching and pinching the mother's hand. I took the boy's hand and I rebuked the devil to flee from him. He went on attacking his mother every few minutes and I continued to rebuke the devil until finally, the boy fell face down on the ground. I bent down and picked him up and started praising the Lord for his deliverance until I woke up. Shortly afterwards, I fell asleep again and saw myself in a labour room with two pregnant women who were in labour; one of them was totally helpless. I told them of my experiences in labour rooms and in hospitals generally. I advised them to always have a family member, a close friend or a personal doctor with them for support whenever in a critical condition. In reality, a certain Dr. Sanya, whom Mike and I had met at the India High Commission in Lagos, advised us to travel with a personal doctor in our quest for a medical solution for Dike.

As I advised these ladies in my dream, one of them who was all alone began to panic, so I moved closer to pacify and encourage her. Suddenly, a baby came out from somewhere. I could not tell if I had delivered the child or if it had been one of the women, but the baby looked like Dike and I took him in my arms. The women said the baby had kidney and liver stones which seemed to cause him to choke. His body was see-through and in the child's abdomen, the stones were in lumps and they appeared in segments. I squeezed the baby's abdomen and ten stones came out. As I continued to squeeze his abdomen, his urine and other shiny abdominal fluids came out and I started praising God. As I praised God in the sub-conscious for the victory over the ailment, I woke up and felt wetness on the bed. As I opened my eyes, I saw that I was clutching Dike and he was stained in highly concentrated urine. I changed his clothes and put a receiving blanket on the bed where the urine had stained.

Once more, those revelations strengthened my faith as I understood we were not fighting alone. I recalled the song that said "the battle would not be easy but it would be worth it." I gave God the glory and majestically moved on into another day hoping that a miracle would occurred in Dike's life. I recalled the scripture where Jesus Christ said:

> "I have told you these things, so that in me you may have peace. In this world you will have trouble. But take heart! I have overcome the world."
> John 16:33

The rest of the day was filled with prayers.

That morning, Covenant Chinonyerem, a pastor who had been in the same entrepreneurial class with Chika and I, called to enquire how Dike was doing and asked me to sow a seed of faith on his behalf. I told Chika to sow a seed into her ministry on Dike's behalf and she did as asked. The Lady called the following day to bless Dike and express her appreciation saying she was surprised and delighted that I actually sowed the seed into her ministry.

Mrs. Udoji came by and gave me some prayer novena for baby Jesus to hold and recite for Dike. I was glad that she had us in her thoughts and prayers and later as I searched the scriptures, I saw the hand of God in all our thoughts and events of the day.

Later that day, I went out with my uncle and aunt to visit my cousin Chukwudi, who was in hospital at the Federal Medical Centre. Whilst there, Chika, Dike's godmother, called and gave the phone to her pastor to pray for Dike. He asked me to take some drinking water and hold in my hand as he prayed and blessed it, after which he asked I give it to Dike to drink.

We prayed before we left the hospital and I made an affirmation that we were going to India on a medical tour and will come back victorious.

Chennai

We finally left Nigeria on the 26th of May 2008, after the 10-day delay in Lagos. Mike had arrived Lagos that morning and we all left that evening. We arrived Chennai at 3.00am on Wednesday the 28th of May. As we collected our luggage, we met an Indian, Reverend Father Xavier, whom we had seen earlier in Lagos during our check-in. We exchanged pleasantries and he told us he would come by the hospital later in the day to check on us.

The Apollo Hospital international patient's office sent a driver to pick us up from the airport. At the hospital, we were given a room at the international patient's wing; the room was quite impressive and the hospital at that hour of the early morning, looked and felt like a hotel. We had a very spacious room with a sofa which doubled as a bed for the attendant. Mike was the patient, while I was his attendant. Dike, on the other hand, was an out-patient but it was a very comfortable arrangement.

In the morning, Mike's surgeon Dr. Saravanah came in with some nurses to welcome us and after they left, Reverend Father Xavier came with his brother Malcom, to see us; we were touched by their hospitality. We got some rest after they left.

That evening, I went into town with the hospital driver who was also called Saravanah, to get some provisions, toiletries and a teether for Dike. I got back to the hospital an hour later and Mike told me the liver specialists had come but would be back in the morning to see Dike. The nurses came back and took Mike for an X-ray while I went to sign the consent papers.

Later that morning, the three doctors came and introduced themselves as the liver surgeons, Dr. Anand Khakar, his colleague Dr. Anand Ramamurthy and Dr. B.K.M. Subramenia, the gastroenterologist. The doctors explained Dike's condition to us; it was same as Dr. Gbobo had explained in Port-Harcourt. They informed us the Kasai procedure, which is the medical intervention before liver cirrhosis sets in, had greatly improved in the past ten years. However, seeing that Dike's liver and spleen were greatly enlarged on examination, they felt he might have come a bit too late as the Kasai procedure is best done at 2 months or earlier.

They scheduled a complete check-up for Dike over the next five days to enable them get a clearer picture of his condition. They also talked about the hope of a parent donating a portion of his liver to the baby. I was delighted on hearing this and it became the ray of hope I needed to strengthen me though the journey.

The doctors came back later with forms for me to fill out for the medical procedure which then cost about $400 (15,000 Rupees). Dike was asked to fast from 10pm till 7am for some of the tests. I prayed for God's grace to enable us get some rest without feeding Dike all night.

I was awake till after midnight. It was my 40th birthday so I spent the hour sending messages to my loved ones back home. Most of them replied my messages and some of them called me. Mike and Dike had slept at 9.45pm but Dike woke up at 1am, very hungry and crying. I carried him round the corridors and to the nurses' station and finally fed him 80mls of water which he hungrily gulped and fell asleep at 2am; he woke up again at 5am.

Mike took him from me and I was able to sleep for an hour and a half. At 7am, I took Dike for a blood test. Our next appointment was at 9.25am but I took him early and was glad they took the sample at

8.30am, after which I took him back to the room, changed and fed him. I slept again while Mike took care of him for I was very tired and jet lagged.

At about 1.30pm, the nurses came and wheeled Mike away for surgery. I was still very sleepy, feeling very unwell and too exhausted to go with him besides I couldn't carry Dike in my fatigued state, so I told him I would be praying for him.

Later that day, the three liver doctors came back and we discussed further. I talked about my experience and the ignorance in handling Dike's condition back home. I asked them about the risks involved and the success rate of transplant cases and they assured me that the results were usually good. I was informed they had scheduled a biopsy for the next day and as there might be some bleeding during and after the procedure, they would have to observe and monitor closely as this was the best way to determine what steps to take in the course of Dike's treatment.

Dr. Subramanian prescribed some medication for Dike and said he will show me how to administer them. We were exhausted and went back up for a nap. The doctor later came back to update me on their findings.

They didn't think Dike had biliary atresia. From the scan, they noted he had a contracted gall bladder and an enlarged liver, but all the vital parts seemed intact which made them rule out biliary atresia. The doctor decided to suspend the biopsy scheduled for the next day but said he would study the scans in detail for more insight. The liver enzyme SGOT was over 400 and he was also going to investigate that.

Dike's vitamin and calcium levels were very low which suggested he was not getting enough nutrients from the breast milk. The doctor suggested looking for a more suitable formula for his feeds. He believed that with the medication, Dike would gain some weight especially as this was his essential period of growth, hoping that the liver had not become cirrhotic.

As we discussed all these, my mind kept on racing and accelerating and I felt we were trying to catch up on time. I felt panicked but knew I could not change anything. I reflected on the ten days we spent in Lagos and wondered, perhaps if we had arrived in Chennai a bit earlier, would the diagnosis have been more optimistic? I prayed for a miracle, I prayed that cirrhosis had not set in as this would complicate issues for us.

I reflected on the last scan we had at the UPTH when the radiologist had said Dike's liver was about 9cm. There was nothing I could do but hand my worries to God. I prayed and gave thanks, affirming that there was hope since God Himself had already shown me some good signs.

Later that night, I went down to the recovery room and saw Mike. The surgery on his elbow was a success and I was so thankful to God. I then went to the pharmacy to get some multivitamins for Dike. Shortly afterwards, Mike's surgeon, Dr. Saravanah came up to tell me how the surgery went. He showed me video clips from his camera. He said he achieved the 110 flex of the hand and he had removed the implant and some pellets within the skin. He said the surgery was even more successful than he and Mike had anticipated. Mike was in deep pain and was later brought back to the room around 8pm. I continued to praise God for the success of the surgery.

On Saturday the 31st of May 2008, Dr. Subramania visited and asked me to make an appointment with the Magnetic Resonate Imaging (MRI) Radiologist, Dr. Chidambaranathan, and also get a urine bag to enable me collect Dike's urine for sampling.

A Nigerian, Mrs. Ngozi Nneji whose husband was a patient in the hospital, had heard about us and came round to visit us. She was in hospital with her husband who had just had heart surgery. We exchanged pleasantries and she was relieved to see people from home as she had been at the hospital for some weeks and found the food inedible. She had felt helpless having no Nigerians to communicate with.

All this while, Dike had become quite irritated. He would scratch his eyes and I was usually scared he would hurt himself so I cut his finger nails quite often. His gums were also very itchy and I gave him a teeter which he chewed quite often. His complexion was becoming lighter and he had patches of red skin all over his body. He would scratch his abdomen, especially in the liver region whenever I exposed him to be changed.

Despite all these changes and the irritation he experienced, the Indians marvelled whenever they saw him. They all loved to play with him, especially one of the sisters called Leema who would occasionally take him to the nurses' station to show him off to the other nurses on duty. The Indian nurses were called Sisters. Dike was usually very charming and smiled a lot. Occasionally, he would cry because he wanted to be carried around or made to stand on my laps while I supported him with my hands.

As the days went by, I once more asked God for a confirmation of what was going on in the midst of my anxiety. On one of those days, my cousin Anyi called and while we talked, I said I believed in miracles but sometimes it is quite confusing when people say that a serious issue is nothing.

Knowing that I am the one facing the challenge and knowing where it pinches, even though I was expectant for a miracle, I was a bit confused when some men of God just dismissed a serious challenge as nothing. I needed to understand if this was an act of faith or a denial of a real challenging situation. I must confess that at this point in time, I had become emotional and once more, had started doubting my faith as I focused on the diagnosis.

As I spoke with my cousin, even with my disbelief and thoughts, I pulled myself together and did not speak about it because I did not want my cousin to have the impression that I had little faith with Dike's challenge. I repented of these negative thoughts, knowing that I needed to hold onto the Lord's report and not focus on the doctor's report or give in to doubts.

Less than an hour later, Dr. Subramania came in to tell me that he did not think Dike had biliary atresia from their temporary findings. I was elated but he then he said there were so many other things that could be wrong and they would diagnose that eventually.

At about 4am, Dike was still awake and as I read the devotional, I was drawn back to the confirmations I received as I constantly asked for revelations. I also needed to be taught the things I needed to learn, so I went back to the devotional of 24th May with the title "Effect of a Report".

I also looked at the reading for the 28th of May 2008 titled "Watch for Signs" with the memory verse being Acts 4:31.

> "And when they had prayed, the place was shaken where they were assembled together; and they were all filled with the Holy Ghost and they spoke the Word of God with boldness."
> Acts 4:31

In the commentary, Pastor Adeboye's stated that the presence of divine fire in your life indicates that your prayers are answered. Many people do not know when to stop praying over issues because they are not sensitive to recognize signs indicating that the prayer has been heard. Jesus said, we should watch and pray; we ought to obey with the action point being - Father, by your Holy Spirit, help me to recognize when You have heard my prayer so that I can thank You.

Reading Joshua 14:6-8 and Numbers 13:27-33 where the spies said they looked like grasshoppers in the sight of the descendants of Anak, we understand that the report we believe determines our end.

If you are failing or retrogressing, it is possible you are holding on to an evil report. Drop it fast. The report you believe is what you will confess and what you confess is what heaven will give to you. In Mark 11:23 Jesus said, "...He shall have whatsoever he saith". Therefore, be careful what you say about yourself especially when you encounter difficulties for it may come to pass!

Never confess what you do not want to possess. Many believers are victims of their confessions and yet they are seriously seeking for non-existent external enemies. Hence the scripture commands us to confess strength when weak, healing when sick and wealth when poor.

God has His own report in any situation. Receiving a divine revelation assists you to believe God's report. Search for His report in the Bible; believe and confess it and it will become your reality.

Reading these texts and meditating on them equipped me for the battle. I chose not to be intimidated by whatever name the doctor gave the ailment they said Dike had. At this point, the doctor said it could be anything but I held unto God's report that Dike was healed in Jesus name. For He said in Isaiah 53:5 that by His stripes we are healed and also in Numbers 14:28.

> "Say unto them, as truly as I live, saith the Lord, as ye have spoken in mine ears, so will I do to you."
> Numbers 14:28.

Through it all the song that kept on warming my heart was the refrain, "For death shall not hold me captive, even in the grave Jesus is LORD".

I thanked God that by the time I had all these revelations, after my myopic view on the stand of the men of God that called Dike's ailment nothing, I started to have a deeper understanding of the things of God from the writings of Pastor Adeboye.

Further Investigations

On Monday the 2nd of June 2008, Dike was scheduled for the MRI scan at 11am and was not allowed to eat from 6 am. He slept hungry and was given a sedative but he woke up and cried for the next thirty minutes. I was therefore asked to feed him, after which we tried to scan him. The very noisy machine woke him up again, so I took him out and fed him, then he slept off again. He was scanned for about eight minutes then he woke again because the mild anesthesia given to him had worn off. It became totally frustrating getting through with the MRI so we were asked to come back the following morning. I felt very upset that he was deprived of food for about six hours when he didn't even need to fast for that scan.

The next day, we went down at 8.40am for the scan and Dike was sedated again. During the procedure, he woke up twice but we were able to finish at 10.30am. I took the next day off to have a medical check which to my utmost amazement cost just about 4,500 rupees (about N18, 000). I was quite impressed with the facilities at the hospital. There were a lot of departments and units that one would never have imagined unless one went there.

Later in the day, the doctor came to give us an update on the MRI. The film showed all the internal organs were okay but the image of the liver was not clear and so they could not get much of the details they were looking for. Therefore, they planned to go ahead with the biopsy and the HIDA scan. All the explanations the doctor made then were too technical for I was mentally and physically fatigued. He wanted the investigations to continue the following day so I left, but still had to go out again to get some basic supplies in preparation for the next day.

The hospital driver took me to a baby shop called Just Born which was within the neighbourhood, and I was able to get the things Dike needed. We went to a grocery shop called Nuts N' Spices and got some provisions and afterwards some basic electrical items.

Back at the hospital, I got some medication including phenobarbitone which the doctor had prescribed for the biopsy. When I got back up to the room, there was no electricity in our wing. I was told that the driver had plugged the adaptor I had bought and it caused a spark, tripping off the electricity. By the time power was restored, I was completely exhausted. I was also very overwhelmed by the update the doctor had given earlier that evening about Dike's condition. The only consolation I had was my Bible, the Open Heavens devotional and my writings.

I had faith that whatever the diagnosis was, the Indian doctors had all the resources, manpower and expertise to treat it, even as I also affirmed that God was the ultimate healer. I felt that we were in the right place at the right time. Mike on the other hand, felt that whatever would be would be and constantly told me to stop worrying about what I had no power to change.

I was fatigued, hungry and irritable and needed a quick bath before falling asleep when I remembered I had to give Dike the phenobarbitone I had just bought. He was already two hour late to taking it in order to dye his liver for the biopsy the following morning as explained by the doctor. Mike and I had actually deliberated on the dosage and he told me to give 2 caps of 5ml but I said I believed I was to give 5 caps of the 5ml. I went ahead and gave 25ml and right after he took the last cup, I looked again at the bottle and saw clearly on the bottle that it was written (25mg to 5ml). I immediately developed a fever and felt faint.

I had mistakenly and ignorantly overdosed him. I landed myself in a nightmarish position. The sleep cleared and I immediately tried to call the doctor to clarify the dosage but could not get through to him. That terrible blunder could have been fatal. I had told Mike just before I administered the medication that everywhere I went that day I had dosed off and as I walked, I felt very faint. I had been totally stressed out and needed to quickly unwind in the shower and then lie down.

I started fretting and had cold sweat all over me. I quickly carried Dike to the nurses' station to report myself as fast as I could. They confirmed my fears and called a paediatrician who came promptly and advised we take him down to the intensive care unit.

We got to the massive first floor emergency wing which looked very unassuming. We located the ICU and the paediatrician on duty took over the case. They promptly put a tube though Dike's nostrils which went into his stomach and with a large syringe quickly sucked out 15mls of the syrup he had ingested. He flushed water into the tube and tried taking more out but this was very slow in coming out. So he attached a bag to enable it come out gradually on its own.

The next procedure was charcoal administration which was pounded in a small mortar and diluted with water, and then injected though the tube in three dozes during the night, at precisely 12 midnight, 3am and 6am.

Dike cried all though the night from hunger, the irritation of the tube in his nostril, his itchy face and having been pricked all over several times to first find a vein to set up a line, and then later for further blood investigations. The pricking continued into the next morning and my heart bled for my poor child.

I watched Dike all night for sleep had at that point, eluded me as pain and anxiety took over my exhausted body. I had a migraine and hàd no medication. I was nauseous and felt empty and frustrated. Yet somehow, I knew that all things concerning Dike's challenge would get to its worst before they began to get better.

Early the next morning I called Dr. Subramania and he was so sorry and commended my quick decision of taking Dike to the ICU. He later came down to see us and asked me not to blame myself for the error. He admitted he had learnt from my mistake, for he never anticipated that a layman could confuse millimetre for milligram and said he would point this out to his colleagues.

In Nigeria, medicine is prescribed in millimetres while Dr. Subramania wrote his prescription in milligrams. This was where I became confused and made the error in the administration of the medication. Mike came down and met us later and the doctor assured us all was fine and that Dike nevertheless, would have still ended up in that same section as he had already been scheduled for a biopsy.

Having gone through so much in the night, the biopsy was postponed to the next day, Thursday the 5th of June 2008. Throughout the day, Dike's blood was taken for different tests. His haemoglobin which was 10.2 g/dL in the night had dropped to 8.2 g/dL during the day, so the doctors decided to give an immediate blood transfusion before the biopsy. When it was time to go into the theatre, I saw Dike to the door and I went back up to be with Mike for a while.

By the time I went back to the theatre, Dike was back to the

ICU and awake. I fed him as instructed by the doctors and he fell asleep. He later become restless from the monitors all wired around him, the tube dropping from his nostril, and the I.V. tube on his wrist in addition to his very itchy face. I had no choice but to handle him with utmost care. He was given pain relievers through the I.V. and I finally was able to sleep with him most of the day but as usual, we were up most of the night.

As I watched him in the two days we spent in the ICU, I observed that he had become very chubby and looked more like his sister Dalu except for his coloured eyes. I could clearly see what the lack of vitamins in his system had reduced him to. His stool remained yellow after he excreted the balls of charcoal he was infused with to mop up all traces of phenobarbitone in his digestive system.

Later that night, I spoke to some of my relatives and I was assured that the family was praying for Dike. I finally slept at 2am and woke at 9.30am.

We awoke into another bright and sunny day. It was a beautiful day. In my challenged state, I had completely blocked out all thoughts of missing our children to enable me cope with the double challenge I faced with Mike and Dike. Mike's surgeon came in and said he will discharge Mike if Dike is given a room the next day since it wouldn't make sense admitting the family in two rooms. Mike had gone for his third day of physiotherapy and his surgery was truly a success story.

Dr. Subramaniam came to see us in the ICU for our discharge and we took photographs with him and Dr. Nathvat, the young ICU attending house officer who did all the procedures on Dike. From their report, Dike's liver was now 11cm, a 2cm increase from what it was a month ago at the University of Port-Harcourt Teaching Hospital, however I did not know if this was good news or bad news. We moved back to Mike's room and I slept a bit. We had a few visitors, and later I went to schedule an appointment for a HYDA scan for Dike.

We met Dr. Saravanah and asked to be discharged since we were all stable enough to check out of the hospital. The international office booked a room for us at the Sea Shell Residency, which is a two-star hotel in the neighborhood of the Apollo Hospital and the hospital driver Saravanah dropped us off.

I was excited when Dike ate his first solid meal on Friday the 6th of June 2008 aged 5 months. On that day, we went to the hospital for Mike's physiotherapy. We also collected some of Dike's medical reports, and Mike went through them and for the first time; the reality of the report hit him. I left him and went into the bathroom to allow him moan over the plight of Dike's medical reports.

My prayer that night was this: "God I do not want to look unto a man's face but to look up to you for the solution we needed for our son".

I was hurting and the thought that came to me that night was that of the various persecutions one faces as a Christian who ought to hold onto his faith. I was very hurt, with a burden in my heart and I was moved to pray. I cried onto God to save me from the emotional hurt I was going through. It was compounded by the doctors' report that Dike would probably not witness his first birthday if nothing was done soon. That night, my heart bled and I recoiled into my shell speaking sparingly, fasting and quietly taking my burden to the Lord in prayer. The cereal and juice Dike took made him stool a lot on Saturday.

On Monday morning, we went to the hospital for the HIDA scan and as usual spent time moving from one section to another, making payments in the billing section, putting the I.V. line on Dike and taking the imaging of 5 films every 2 hours. A typical day in the hospital was extremely hectic, but the level of efficiency was overwhelming despite the large number of patients encountered at each section of the hospital.

In the evening, we decided to treat ourselves to something different from the meals we had been eating. Our new friend, Jithu in the International Department arranged for us to eat at a five-star hotel and the driver took us there for a buffet. The night out was a killjoy and the food though nice, was Indian. Not liking spicy food, I did not enjoy the spices used in the Indian meals we ate; we returned to the hotel and I slept, very frustrated.

The next day, we went back to the hospital and spent time at the international office with Jithu Jose and his colleagues as usual. He helped me download some pictures from my camera and burn them into a CD for which I was grateful. He was generous in making our stay comfortable and worthwhile. I met some Nigerian ladies from Abuja, including Dr. Uju Bosah from the National Hospital in Abuja. We chatted and exchanged phone numbers and we have both remained close till date.

Anxiety

I was on the brink of tears. Tuesday came and went. I had been given an injection on my Achilles heel which had been aching due to tendonitis. I had done a lot of walking in the past weeks and this had worsened my ankle pain and so I sought Mike's doctor for treatment. A few months after my first daughter Ugonna was born, I had a similar pain in my wrist and was told it was tendonitis. Dr. Yellowe in Port Harcourt gave me an injection on the spot where there was pain and that cured it. He explained that pregnancy was responsible for the pain which was caused by the inflammation of the joint; it could also be caused due to the result of the body adjustments while shedding the excess fluid when a baby is birthed.

With Dr. Yellowe's explanation, I was not surprised when this occurred again after Dike's birth but I thanked God the pain stopped. Both doctors who treated me had said that if the injection was not given at the location of the pain, the treatment would not work. Doctor Saravanah advised I wear wedged shoes that had a bit of a heel to ease the strain and pain.

After the treatment, I collected all the outstanding medical reports to enable us consult with the specialists. We saw Dr. Subramaniam again and took the HIDA scan to Dr. Ramamuthy. He looked at the scan and explained to us that there was a total blockage of Dike's gall bladder.

I was still in a lot of pain from the injection in my heel and with the loss of hope the doctors pronounced, I was all in tears. Despite my downcast spirit, Mike and I managed to have dinner at a roadside Chinese restaurant as we left the hospital. We just needed the food to survive and there was nothing we understood from the entire menu we were presented with.

That evening, we changed our room to a better one having complained of cockroaches and a broken window. Dike and I managed to play into the night. There were times when Dike was cheerful enough to play and these were my most memorable times with him; it also made me very emotional. I could not understand why a handsome child, who could sometimes be so cheerful, would be given a death sentence. I just wanted to save my little child in any way I could, so I trusted the Lord with all my heart that the solution would come someday in an unprecedented manner.

Despite my play with Dike that night, his eyes had become very irritated. We finally slept and he awoke after just two hours itchy and scratching all over as usual. I wept as Dike scratched himself especially his eyes, with vengeance and I prayed once more for God to give him peace through this challenge. I always prayed for peace and God always gave it to me; this was the most singular reason why I kept on keeping on in faith.

Dike's blood had a lot of issues at this point and the doctor was very concerned about it. I brought out his file that night to check and arrange all the reports in the right order. I become alarmed as I went through his reports and saw that the alkaline phosphates had shot up from 111 to over 1600. I recalled that the paediatric surgeon in Port Harcourt had told me that if this figure exceeded 1000 then it meant the liver was completely blocked. I then had another reminder that delay is truly dangerous.

Once again, I began to blame myself for all the delays and wondered what I had been waiting for in Port Harcourt and in Lagos just three weeks earlier. I was even more alarmed because that report was done on the 28th of May, a day before my birthday and I never really studied it until that night, the 10th of June. Many thoughts crossed my mind and it felt justified by the bad report of the biopsy. I could not wait to experience the miracle of restoration of Dike's health. I was anxious to hear from the surgeon the next day whilst worrying about anything I could imagine.

Dike was all yellow and itchy, not gaining weight and had a distended stomach like a child suffering from kwashiorkor. I had to reaffirm to myself that I still trusted in God and rebuked the devil that he will not get my son.

As I tuned the television to The God Channel that day, I was delighted to watch a programme with Joyce Meyer. It seemed to me like a miracle had just happened; I felt like I had hit the jackpot.

"We should not allow the devil to steal our hope because help was on its way," said Meyer.

I held onto this prophecy.

We later went to see the doctors and while we waited at the reception, our Indian friend Nathalie came and pacified me for about an hour. She was truly the great pillar I needed at that low moment in my life; she told me her husband Ken and their eight year old son Joshua whom they also called Nathan could not wait to meet us.

We finally saw the doctors and we were advised to get MCT oil and some steroids to enable Dike gain some weight. They confirmed that the liver was at its threshold and would definitely need a transplant. I spent the day crying as the doctors spoke to us and I was bruised over and over; we seemed to be battling against all odds. Mike was already in deep pain, going through the guilt and torment of his son's ailment. He was afraid of another major surgery, having just come out of surgery which had seen him in and out of the theatres about four times in the past ten years.

I told him that it was okay, that he did not have to donate and I did not want him hurt any more than he was. What I had to deal with at that period would remain the lowest ebb of my life.

After we saw the liver specialists, we went to get some milk and juice from the local supermarket. I was dropped off with Dike at the Sea Shell Residency for a short while before going back to the hospital for our next appointment for the day.

We saw the haematologist Dr. Raj who saw me so weepy and asked what the doctor had said to me that put me in such a mood. I explained Dike's situation and that it made me so anxious. If we had knowledge of the situation in his first few weeks of life, we would not be talking about a liver transplant by this time.

I had blamed myself for all the delays in getting treatment, but was greatly relieved when Dr. Raj told me not to be too hard on myself because most babies who go in for the Kasai procedure do not even have a successful outcome. Only about twenty percent of Kasai procedures were successful and most of these successful ones would probably still need a liver transplant by age 18.

She advised me to be a pillar of strength and told me she learnt a great lesson from a lady who came to the Apollo Hospital with her son who required a bone marrow transplant. The lady and her son had come from East Africa and stayed for a long time, but she had stubborn faith in their hopeless situation.

She had finally found favour in God's eyes and left with her son after a successful bone marrow transplant. Dr. Raj was convinced it was successful partly because of the woman's prayers and her unshakeable faith. Dr. Raj is Hindu but here she was telling me the encouraging story of a Christian woman and that she had learnt to be brave by listening and being a consultant to them. She asked me to cultivate such stubborn faith; I left her feeling much better.

I will forever remember this encounter with Dr. Raj and the effect of her encouraging words on me. The story and her belief that prayers work with faith above all things as the antidote for anxiety, was quite phenomenal and I tapped into that energy.

As I wrote about my daily encounter, Dike was on my laps cooing and I just beheld the little boy in his handsomeness despite his severe weight lost. I thanked God for the beauty of His son who I was privileged to hold in my arms.

I received additional comfort from my aunties and cousins who called me continually, upholding us in prayers as we faced this challenge. There were days I became demoralized but these conversations reminded me that we were not alone in our prayers and such encouragement was what I needed to keep my faith and trust in God.

On Thursday, we went back for some blood tests. Later, Dr. Subramaniam gave some vaccines and updated Dike's vaccine chart. We had deliberately omitted taking some of these vaccines in Nigeria as my aunt, Dr. Nwosu had advised us to leave the rest of the vaccines to the Indian doctors who would know better on what to give and how to administer it.

We saw the dietician next and she recommended a formula called Dexolac for Dike. Later that night, I had phone calls again from my cousins, Chizoba and Adaeze, my brother Tonye and later my uncle Agunze who always emphasized the good virtues of a wife and mother in me. I truly appreciated his words which continually encouraged me to remain strong and keep faith.

Chizoba advised me to pray with Mike and anoint Dike every two hours for the next two days. It was a very hectic day for us but we finally got some quiet time to pray in the hotel room at about 11pm.

We had more telephone calls that night from my cousin Obinna, who share the same birthday with me, and Aunty Ida, my mother's twin sister. It was midnight in India but early evening in Nigeria. Despite my tiredness, these phone calls made me realise all the more that we were not alone through this travail.

Dike had taken the Dexolac and it was very good for his system. He stooled several times and it looked close to normal, much better than it had been in the past months. I prayed he would add some weight soon as he weighed a mere 5.1 kg. I was not very excited about this, but despite all his challenges, Dike remained a smiling child, to the glory of God.

On the 12th of June 2008, I had minor surgery to remove the

warts on my face. I was happy to have found a solution to the invasion on my face over the past four years. I was so relieved when Dr. Ramachandra said he would use a laser to burn them off. They were over a hundred spots and to my greatest amazement, the procedure cost me only 1,000 rupees which was the equivalent of 3,000 Naira, about thirty dollars at the going exchange rate.

We went to the bookshop and bought some books, for I always make it a point of duty to buy books anywhere I travelled to. I value reading, especially when I feel low in spirit and need a boost. We left the hospital bookshop and decided to walk back to the hotel through a back road. Along the road we were delighted to discover a beautiful restaurant which was a favourite hangout for the young people whom we presumed to be the children of the elites in Chennai.

We were so glad to finally treat ourselves to a decent meal in weeks. It was relatively expensive but we were glad we could afford it, especially having been starved for weeks of the sort of meals we desired. We decided to eat there once daily for the rest of our stay in Chennai.

We got back to our hotel in the dark and for the first time since we got to Chennai, ate well and had a good rest into mid-morning of Saturday.

Help On Its Way

We finally reached another major junction in our journey with Dike. It had become obvious to me that the doctors at the Apollo Hospital at that time had no solution for Dike. I had wept my heart out especially when they advised us to take him back home and bring him back in three months' time for a liver transplant. They had also said his weight was too low to undergo a successful liver transplant, a mere 5.1 kg at 6 months of age.

My worry then was that if they could not keep him and fatten him up, why would they advise us to take him home, find a donor and come back in three months' time? I felt they had given him a death sentence, but the Lord still reassured me that He had not resigned on Dike's matter, therefore we should not rely only on the doctor's report.

As we pondered on the facts before us, Tonye called and he told us that since we were against all odds and did not have visas to the UK or the USA, we might as well consider a second opinion there in India.

After we spoke, Mike and I unanimously agreed to ask Nathalie who had earlier hinted that if we needed a second opinion, she could find a referral for us. I called her immediately.

"Praise God! Praise God!!"

This was Nathalie's response on hearing our request. She told me her husband and their son Joshua had been praying for Dike every day and looked forward to meeting us. She assured us that her husband would come on Saturday morning to take us to the Child Trust Hospital. We had a plan!

On Saturday morning, Ken came in a taxi to take us to Child Trust Hospital. We met with the paediatricians on duty; they took all the relevant information for their records and asked us to come back on Monday morning to see the gastroenterologist. Dike weighed 5.5kg on their manual scale which put a little smile on my face.

On Sunday, we stayed indoors and slept most of the day from exhaustion. Later, we went to the Euro Restaurant and while there, my aunt Dr. Nwosu called, her daughter Jacqueline also called from Aberdeen. They were saddened by the news of our hoping against all odds. My cousin Dike and his wife Yetunde also called from the USA later that night. Dike wept when I told him of his little boy's plight. For the first time, I heard Dike break down in sobs for his godson. The day was Sunday the 15th of June 2008.

After the phone calls, I turned on the television and tuned to the God Channel. John Hagee was ministering and we called the prayer line where a lady prayed for us. She said they will pray for 30 days and that the result will end well. Mike told me he had also called some prayer help lines. After I spoke to Yetunde, sleep still eluded me as I pondered on the way forward with our son.

It finally dawned on me that in the past few days, I had been acting without faith. The doctors' reports were tormenting me and had taken over my reasoning and judgment. So I resolved not to say anything about a transplant anymore but to just dwell on Dike being on medication and on a special diet. I felt better after this resolution to change my mind-set which was not a denial, but a new interpretation and a positive mental attitude towards the challenge at hand.

At 2am, my friend Bassey Fiebai called from Port Harcourt to say she had been praying for us and was about to go to bed. She had spoken to Mike a few days earlier and he had told her about the transplant. Afterwards, I told Mike that we had not done our best in finding a solution to Dike's ailment for we knew he has a destiny for his life and his names were prophetic, "Diken'agha" meaning "the mighty warrior in battle" and "Kenechukwu" meaning "thanks to God". I reaffirmed to Mike that after the battle is fought and won, we would thank God.

We were awake most of the night but finally returned to sleep in the early hours of the morning. Mike woke me shortly after to get ready for the appointment at Child Trust Hospital despite my fatigued state. We got to the hospital and did the preliminary checks before meeting the elderly and experienced paediatric gastroenterologist with an amazing name and looks. Dr V.S. Sankaranarayaran was stocky but heavily built with the typical Indian looks of a wise guru. For some reason, his countenance left a lasting impression on Mike and I.

Dr. V.S.S, as I would call him, asked his attending physician questions pertaining to Dike's records and the results of the Apollo Hospital investigations. When the doctor said biliary atresia with an advice of a transplant, Dr. V.S.S. snapped. He studied the blood reports and said he disagreed with their diagnosis. He asked us when we noticed the changes in Dike's stool and urine colour. I said about one month after his birth but was not really too sure since there were usually changes in the stool of babies at infancy especially with Dike's yellow stool that gradually become very oily and then beady.

He told me that from the facts I had given and from the blood analysis, he disagreed with the Apollo Hospital. He asked me to put Dike on the examination table then he put on his hand gloves to induce stool. He saw the stool and said he was still convinced this was not a case of biliary atresia.

Dr. V.S.S. asked us how and why we came to the Child Trust Hospital and we told him about Ken and Nathalie whose nephew received kidney treatment in their care and was doing fine. The doctor told us he would do his very best to find out exactly what was wrong with Dike and inform us the next day.

A group of medical students came in whilst he was attending to us, and he lectured them on Dike's ailment and his diagnosis as against the previous diagnosis. We were so impressed and saw this encounter with Dr. V.S.S. as the intervention that we needed to change the report we did not want to hear. We witnessed the grace of God in our greatest time of need and confusion.

He asked for the scan results and we brought out the HIDA scan and were surprised when he said it was outdated. We were most amazed that such equipment existed having only seen one for the first time at Apollo Hospital, and yet this wonder of a machine was flawed by Dr. V.S.S.'s interjection that he did not even want to see the report.

He asked if another abdominal scan was done after Dike ate and I said no. He seemed more interested in the inconsistency in the bilirubin level, alkaline phosphates, the rest of the liver cells and some other blood issues only he understood in-depth. We could connect with him because in Apollo, these were the same factors the doctors had pondered on. They wondered why Dike's blood continued breaking down until they finally concluded it was due to the lack of essential vitamins.

Even from my lay man's view, I knew these were the factors that needed to be investigated thoroughly, and we were most assured when Dr. V.S.S. pointed this out and said he would look deeper into it, refusing to make a biased decision even from the biopsy report. He said there was no liver cirrhosis and that he knew other things were wrong with Dike but he did not believe it was extrahepatic biliary atresia.

He delivered this judgment as if he was in a court of law with a gavel in his hand, thereby sentencing the previous reports and reporters to jail. We, being the audience were euphoric at the judgment of hope; we now had our second opinion. At last, someone with great experience was asking the right questions and this gave us so much hope and joy for the next day, at least.

Dr. V.S.S. sent me to the radiology department to do an abdominal scan for Dike with the assurance that the radiologist on duty was a man with vast experience and would give an accurate result of his findings. He also asked us to do the liver enzyme tests in a specialist laboratory which was a walking distance from the Child Trust Hospital in Nungambakkam. We were to collect the reports and take to him the next day. He advised that we discard all medication Dike was on and purchase the ones he would prescribe.

Some of the medication he prescribed we already had from Apollo Hospital, except for Rifampicin suspension which he explained was to flush the liver. The other medication were Zincovit multivitamin syrup and Ondansetron oral solution to reduce the itching and to stop the vomiting, Evion drops for the vitamin D deficiency and Udiliv D.T for the liver restoration. Dike was already on Vitamin as prescribed by Dr. BMK. Mike and I left in excitement and felt very positive at what fate had for Dike after our consultation with Dr. V.S.S.

As we waited for the radiologist's call, I could not hide my joy and thankfulness to God for the ray of hope we had just found. I said a prayer of thanksgiving right there, in appreciation for the peace He brought our way. I felt as if the Holy Spirit had descended on me like it did on the apostles of Jesus while they waited in the upper room on the day of Pentecost (Acts 2).

Interestingly, the hospital was filled with different Indian gods and idols; there was even a shrine at the entrance with its high priest visibly present. Yet, I was very comfortable as moved by the Holy Spirit to pray at that time. I asked God to have mercy on little Dike as he had suffered in the hands of doctors and nurses, laboratory attendants and radiologists, and fasted so much from birth. In the Bible, Jesus told his disciples that a certain type of challenge could only be solved with prayers and fasting. (Matthew 17:21) so we keyed into this with Dike.

God's ways are not our ways, and at the time I was writing this journal, I did not know that God had already answered our prayer. I had a sudden burst of joy after that prayer and instantly knew all would be well. I had no idea that we still had a long journey ahead of us and the suffering would be much more than we could imagine. Still, I had the assurance that help was on its way.

As we left the hospital, we could barely wait for the next day to come. Dr. V.S.S. told us not to worry when we saw the colour of Dike's urine was red as this was caused by the medication Rifampicine. He had even taken pictures of Dike's stool and urine with his camera after he induced Dike to "pass some motion" as they call stool in India.

At the end of the day, we felt most fulfilled and grateful for the joy and hope the day had brought us at the Child Trust Hospital, which also was known locally as the Kamchi Kamokoti Children's Hospital. Mike was also excited that the hospital is one of the beneficiaries of his Rotary International club. Truly God had used Christian believers to bring the good news to us and we remained truly grateful for His grace on our beloved son's life.

Tuesday the 17th of June 2008. We went to see Dr. V.S.S. and he asked for Dike's blood to be taken for more investigations. He gave Dike injections of vitamin A and vitamin D3. Dike's bilirubin report on Monday had dropped to 18.6u/moL/L conjugated and 11.5 u/moL/L for the direct. The alkaline phosphates had also dropped to 455 from 1008 in the last one week. We were truly excited at this improvement. We also noticed that his abdomen had reduced in size. Dr. V.S.S took pictures of Dike, insisting that his chin and jaw were normal like a healthy baby's. He looked at his ears and other parts of his body and said he was still convinced the baby did not have biliary atresia. We did an x-ray of the spine and he requested we get the slide of the biopsy from the Apollo Hospital. He wrote a letter to the pathologist for this request which we took with us.

We made photocopies of all Dike's reports and attached them to the file with Dr. V.S.S. and we left feeling more fulfilled than ever. We had lunch at our favourite restaurant, Piccolo in Nungambakkam and then we went back to the hotel. I spoke to Sylvia, Chika Peterside and Mrs. Ajuebon the Proprietress of our children's school. I slept late as usual, though not by choice.

Dike passed stool ten times or more daily which was quite exhausting for it meant constant diaper changes and several feeds in between. Sometimes it could be so frustrating watching Mike sleep while I handled Dike till the early mornings when we would both fall asleep exhausted. Despite this challenge, I felt joyful seeing Dike smile and watching him crawl around with a good demeanour except when the itching drove him nuts. I still did not consider him sick but just challenged by an ailment that only God could reverse.

On Wednesday evening, we went to Child Trust Hospital for Dike's ECHO after staying indoors all day. Mike had gone to Apollo Hospital to collect the biopsy slide from the pathologist. I called Mrs. Nneji; she told me her husband had had a seizure that evening on their way home after they had gone to the Emirates office to change their tickets to enable them leave on Friday. He was rushed in an ambulance back to the theatre, thus aborting their travel plans. She was confused and I urged her to find a quiet place to pray, after Mike and I had prayed with her. I called her later that night at about 10pm when her husband had just come out of surgery and was being transferred to the Intensive Care Unit. We thanked God for another successful day in delivering her husband from death and for giving her hope.

Dike vomited all night, so on Thursday we went back to Child

Trust Hospital. We were not certain why that happened, perhaps as a result of the capsule the doctor prescribed. It had been a difficult night and we slept exhausted at about 6a.m. We woke up at 10.30am when Chizoba Onuoha called.

We told the doctor our plight and he removed the capsule from Dike's medication, prescribing three other drugs in addition to the cocktail of five. Thereafter, we went back to the Apollo Hospital for Dr. Subramania's appointment. He talked to us on the possibility of a liver transplant and I told him that I had confidence that there might be no need for a transplant. On the spur of the moment, I asked of his religion and he said he was Hindu. I also asked if he thought anything else could be wrong with Dike.

"Not to the best of his knowledge," was his response.

Mike asked Dr. Subramania if there was any medication that could cure Dike, especially one that could flush out his bilirubin but the doctor replied there was none for Dike's situation. This was a concern, and we decided not to tell him that we had sought for a second opinion. We left him and I went to see Jithu Jose at the International Wing, to help send pictures to my mail box so I could forward them to our friends and family back home. Mike went for his physiotherapy and afterwards came to meet me there.

I suffered a migraine and Jithu ordered a chicken sandwich for me, which was a most welcome change. I found out it was ordered from the restaurant in the hospital. I ate some, leaving some for Mike. From then on, I occasionally bought the delicacy. We left Jithu's office and, as I was still feeling very sick and nauseous from the migraine, Mike had to hold me until we caught our usual ride on a three wheeler back to our hotel.

In the midst of this, we were excited because on that day, Thursday June 19th 2008, Dike began to sit up unaided.

I got up early and read my Open Heavens devotional for that day titled "Hooked on Wrong Choices". The memory verse was Philippians 4:6:

> "Be careful for nothing; but in everything by prayer and supplication with thanksgiving let your requests be made known unto God."
> Philippians 4:6

Dr. V.S.S. had asked us if we had noticed any change in Dike. We responded that his skin, which had grown so dark, had come back to its normal light complexion. His stool was looking more normal and his urine was much lighter in colour as well. It was also obvious that the distended abdomen had shrunk and he no longer itched. The doctor asked if we were happy with the observations and we answered in the affirmative.

He induced some stool from Dike's rectum and confirmed what he had first told us, which was that Dike did not have biliary atresia but a liver condition called PFIC 2 which was treatable with medication. If cirrhosis sets in however, then a transplant would become inevitable. He explained that there was also the PFIC 1 which unfortunately was not treatable with medication, but from his investigations and Dike's physical appearance, he was most certain that what we were dealing with was not biliary atresia.

This diagnosis for us became the miracle we needed, and we became convinced that all was well and that we had finally reached a destination called Hope. Despite clearly understanding that our journey was nowhere near its destination, we rode on our new found hope that at least we were heading in the right direction. This feeling changed everything for the better, at least for the next few months.

After we left Dr. V.S.S, we discussed our dismay that Dr. Subramania had examined Dike and had asked several questions about his health, his ability to coo and other reflexes, yet did not realise the changes in his physical appearance especially his abdomen which did not look so distended anymore. Mike and I actually hoped there would no longer be a need for a liver transplant which was a clear state of denial.

In fairness to Dr. Subramania, he was an experienced gastroenterologist. He had practiced in the U.K. and had just moved back to India to help add value to the medical field in his country. I liked him very much and had a very good rapport with him. He was very kind and gentle and very pathetic to our case. He had done the best he could with the diagnosis, recommending feeds and necessary medication to make Dike comfortable and also enable him grow a bit in preparation for a liver transplant.

We spent the weekend at the Emirates office to arrange documents for travelling back home. On Sunday the 22nd June 2008, Ken, Nathalie and Joshua took us to worship with them at the Assemblies of God Pentecostal Church. I was so tired and in so much pain for I did not get to sleep much the night before; I had carried Dike while sitting up to snooze most of the night. After the service, we were introduced to the pastor and he prayed for Dike. It had been an interesting spirit filled service. We had lunch afterwards in a Chinese restaurant and took beautiful photographs for posterity.

Chennia is the capital of Tamil Nandu in the southern region of India. The language spoken is Tamil and they are mostly Christians.

After Jesus Christ's resurrection and ascension, while his disciples went to spread the Gospel of Christ throughout the old world, Thomas, his disciple went to a region of India and established the church. He was later made a Saint and became St. Thomas, but popularly referred to as Saint Tom in Chennai where he lived the rest of his life. He was buried in the St. Thomas Church in Chennai which he built and it remains a historic structure till date.

On a later trip to Chennai, Nathalie and her family took Dike and I to the beach and showed us the St. Thomas Church where the tomb of St. Thomas was. It was remarkable hearing such foundational story of our Christendom. More baffling is the fact that despite the early presence of the church in Chennai, a little less than 1% of the over 1.5billion Indians are Christians.

We returned to our hotel room and slept all evening. We finally got up at 9pm when my brother Yemi called me from Lagos and later my cousin Ifenlota also called from Chicago.

Monday the 23rd of June 2008. We went back for our appointment with Dr. V.S.S. He told us that he examined the biopsy film and he was certain that Dike did not have biliary atresia but some other issue with the liver which blocks the flow of the bilirubin. He said the drugs he had prescribed would make the bile flow out. He asked us to see him again on Thursday, with the test results he planned for us to do the following day being Wednesday.

Dr. V.S.S. called Dr. Shobana Rajendran, the paediatrician who had seen us the first day we visited Child Trust. He asked her to examine Dike but Dike would not let her examine him. We went back on Wednesday for some more tests; Dr. Shobana, another female paediatrician and one of their senior colleagues put Dike on their table; surprisingly Dike allowed her to examine him for a long time.

We left the hospital in a good mood and went to Spencer's Mall to shop. Mike bought me some wristwatches and some jewellery. The diamond ring I saw and liked did not fit and I truly wanted a new ring to compliment my single wedding band which looked too plain. We went to the Apollo Hospital on Thursday and we saw Mr. Nneji's doctor friend Dr. Moha, whom Mr. Nneji had advised us to see should we seek for a solution in Japan, North Korea or New Delhi, if we eventually required a liver transplant for Dike. We went back to Dr. V.S.S. and he gave us a report for our doctor in Nigeria. I asked him some questions which I had written down and he answered them all to my satisfaction.

He told us he would keep the biopsy slide for his research and explained that Dike had a congenital problem from birth and that any other children we would have will most definitely end up with similar medical challenges. I quickly told him that I had no intention of having any more children and had even tied my tubes. He explained that the condition of Dike's liver is like a traffic jam where the channels are narrow and the bilirubin manufactured is unable to flow out easily. He believed that the medication he had prescribed of which Dike was already on, will help to open up those channels or create new channels of outflow.

We left Dr. V.S.S. and went back to Spencer's Mall to shop for the ring I desired so much. We finally saw and bought the one I wanted - a beautiful eternity ring with the double rings and diamonds which matched my wedding ring. We shopped for things for the children, bought more formula and medication for Dike, then went back to the hotel to pack for our trip home. The driver Saravanah picked us from the hotel at 12.30am on that Friday, 27th of June and we were off.

We departed Delhi at 4.50am and arrived Dubai at 7.30am. The flight back to Nigeria was smooth and we arrived Lagos on schedule at 2.00pm on Saturday 28th June. Dike and I went to my Uncle's house in Ikoyi where we were well received by family and friends while Mike continued to Port Harcourt. We spent two days in Lagos to enable us testify to family and friends about God's goodness and faithfulness in our lives.

Open Heavens

Whilst in Lagos, I had planned to take Dike to testify at the house fellowship Tonye coordinated which held in Brother Nnaife and Sister Miebi's Victoria Garden City home. However, the plan changed when Tonye called on Sunday afternoon after service informing me he was on his way to see me with a message from Pastor E.A. Adeboye.

My close friend Chichi and her daughter Odero came to see us, and while my aunt and I hosted them, Tonye came in with his message from Pastor E. A. Adeboye. It was a message of hope for Dike's restoration. He gave me a handkerchief which he had sent to Daddy G.O. who was in the U.S.A on a visit. The handkerchief had been blessed and sent back that morning. Tonye said he would not be at the house fellowship as I had thought, but was having lunch with the celebrated Minister of God, motivational speaker and bestselling author Dr. Myles Monroe who was visiting from the Bahamas as the guest minister at their City of David parish. We went outside and took photographs with Tonye before he hurriedly left for his appointment. He asked me not to worry about our inability to attend the house fellowship for there would be many more opportunities to testify in the near future. Sadly, Dr. Myles Munroe died with his wife Ruth in a plane crash on the 9th of November 2014.

We left for Port Harcourt the next day and while in the aircraft, I brought out the Open Heavens devotional to read Sunday's message which I had not read on Sunday, and right there before me was yet another confirmation of God's promise regarding our challenge. The devotion for the day was titled "It's About to Rain". In the message, Daddy G.O. said that not long ago, he had just returned from a trip to the U.S.A and a sister came to him with a request for prayers. The lady's grandmother had a surgery but the incision had refused to heal. The doctors had told them that death was inevitable. Daddy G.O said he was very tired and could not make the trip to go pray for the lady's grandmother. Rather, he chose to bless a handkerchief because he believed that God can use any object for divine healing. The lady took the blessed handkerchief and placed it on her grandmother's abdomen. The next day, the incision was totally healed and there was no scar to show that any surgery had been done.

On reading this message, I shouted for joy for this was the same message entry for the Sunday Tonye delivered the white handkerchief to me. Open Heavens devotional had proven to be a source of encouragement for me at the time of need. I claimed the result that was professed in the scripture and left all to God.

We had a joyous reception in Port Harcourt, and I gave glory to God for bringing us home safely with great hope and expectation. I had no doubt that our tomorrow would be alright.

On Wednesday the 2nd of July 2008, we all flew to Abuja for our interview with the US embassy. We stayed with my Aunt May. When we went for the interview at the American Embassy, the man who interviewed us kept asking why we had our children in the USA. He asked if I was pregnant to which I responded with a loud "No!", and even held up Dike, informing him that I had no intention to have more children and had just returned from India a few days back from a medical trip. He repeatedly told us not to go near any hospital on our next visit especially to have more children. Satisfied, he asked us to pick up the visas the following week.

We went to a restaurant in Wuse2 to order lunch and took the food back to my aunt's house. After lunch, we rested a while before going back to the embassy for Ugonna's USA Passport renewal. That done, we left the embassy very elated having achieved all we needed in Abuja.

It was a beautiful day and we decided to spend the rest of the day house hunting. We had made up our minds to relocate to Abuja in the month Dike was born. We saw a few houses in Wuse and finally chose a duplex in Gwarimpa. We made a down payment on the rent and went home to my Aunt's. It was an exhilarating day and we thanked God for it.

The Second Dream – My Tommorow Shall Be Alright

That afternoon, I had an early evening nap waking up after about an hour and half to find Dike drenched in his own sweat as a result of his condition and the cocktail of medication he took. His body was cold so I took off his shirt and rubbed some powder all over his body then breast fed him. While he sucked, I drifted again into dream land.

I saw a lady who looked like a nurse and an aroma therapist. She asked me about Dike's condition and I told her my fears. She took him from me and said I should watch the procedure she would perform on him. She put one hand on his chest and the other on his lower stomach and squeezed both towards the middle as if she was squeezing the liver. His body became roundish like that of an amoeba and I became worried that he would be hurt, but she told me not to worry.

She squeezed him again then relaxed a bit. She squeezed him a few more times before she got him back into shape. She said this procedure would help to circulate the bile that was trapped in his liver and open up the ducts for an outflow.

She did this procedure all over again and Dike screamed that he could no longer feel sensation in his right leg. We feared she might have touched the sciatic nerve while compressing him. But again she said I should watch her. She took Dike's leg and felt for a specific spot below his feet. She put her thumb on that spot and pressed it very hard, and then she began to massage it. Dike screamed. She then said I should see for myself that Dike was alright. With this, I began rejoicing and praising God. As she squeezed him, I broke out in an intense prayer for the physical manifestation of the angelic visitation and also for the special assignment for Dike's life.

I had hope after this revelation as I remembered that my maternal grandmother, Anuenyi, had often experienced such angelic visitations while she suffered some serious ailments. Until her death in December 2013 at the age of a hundred, she remained in great health but for her last two years when she finally succumbed to the wear and tear of old age. I declared the blessing of longevity on Dike's life as I awoke from my dream.

My prayer point for the day was, "Father, the miracle You have started in Dike's life will come to a true manifestation so that we all will know You clearly as I reaffirmed that Dike's ailment was not unto death as Jesus said in John 11: 4, but for the glory of God that the Son of God may be glorified through it".

I prayed that the unbelievers will come to the Father, the idol worshippers will worship Him and Dike would live to fulfil God's work in his life's journey. Before I got up, I saw once more a flash of Nathalie as the angel who had visited Dike, and she assured me not to worry about his sweating because it was a process of detoxification of Dike's liver.

As I lay on the bed with the sleeve of my shirt drenched in Dikes sweat, I continued to praise God for His revelation that brought me so much comfort and gave me hope to strengthen my faith in the challenge we faced. The date was Wednesday, 9th July of 2008 and I believed God for Dike's perfect restoration.

We went back to Port Harcourt and visited the doctor at the Omega Children's Hospital where we ran some tests. Dike's blood test showed that the liver enzymes were still high but the other blood tests were very good and within range. It was not as alarming as it had been at the time of the initial diagnosis, but the doctor treated him for malaria.

When I took Dike to see Dr. Ekeoku, he reaffirmed his belief just as the Apollo Hospital doctors had diagnosed; it was a possible 80% biliary atresia and 20% giant cell issues. As he spoke, I reaffirmed to myself that I did not care what the doctor's report was but I chose to hold on to my faith as I was only interested in the heavenly doctor's report. Meanwhile, Dike looked so good and played so well.

On the 13th of July 2008, I slept in the early morning and once again dreamt that Dike took another blood test and the result was fair just as it had been in reality in the past week. Then suddenly, a lady called me to say that the result of the test had changed. I asked how come it had changed and she said I should check the readings. I did and I was amazed that the bilirubin had come down from the previous week's 100 to 25 and the SGOT and SGPT read 0 and 1 respectively.

As I looked at the chart in my dream, I began screaming and praising God. In my hysteria, I fainted. After a while, some people helped me up from the floor and asked me to go into the inner room to see the lady boss who had a fruit supplement which I was to give to my baby. I walked into the room and saw a lot of people who had all been healed of different ailments. They had also come to receive the fruit punch and different juice cocktails for cleansing and detoxifying their bodies.

Once again, I was awed by these revelations; the lady looked like Nathalie. The Open Heavens devotional for that Sunday the 13th of July 2008 was titled "Attitude determines Altitude" with the text taken from Genesis 18: 17–19. The message started with some questions - "Does God entrust you with divine secrets? Can He vouch for your character? May He find you trustworthy to bear His mysteries from today in Jesus' name. What did Abraham do to become a storehouse of God's secrets? It was recorded in the text that he adopted a positive attitude that compelled God to fulfil His promises in his life. Once more I claimed Dike's healing.

Within the week, Dike became sick and vomited the Amoxil he was taking for a cough and the Coartem which was given to him for malaria. We were both treated for malaria but I took him back to the hospital and the Amoxil was changed to another medication.

I took the children to C & C Opticians for our second daughter Amaka to have her eyes checked. The doctor was amazed that Amaka had such poor eyesight and exclaimed we should have brought her sooner. She prescribed a pair of glasses immediately for her. While she was doing this, I suddenly realised that for a few days, I had forgotten to give Dike the Ondansetron medication which doubly functioned as anti-itch and anti-vomiting syrup. I had forgotten to replace the empty bottle in his medicine box and since he was taking about thirteen different medications, I had forgotten that one because I had also failed in doing a daily log to check his medication intake.

I felt terrible but thanked God that I realised my short coming. All along, I had thought the Coartem and Amoxil had made him vomit and even asked the doctor to change the Amoxil which was very bitter and very unsmooth. Little did I realise that the Ondansetron I had skipped was the problem.

As the weeks progressed, Mike and I discussed a possible trip to the United State as we all had our visas. We also planned our move to Abuja right after we returned. I made plans for my friend Betty to furnish the Abuja house while we were away to enable us move in immediately we returned.

Journey To The Heart

As I read the daily devotional for 10th of July 2008 written by Melody Beattie titled "Journey to the Heart", I recorded it in my journal for it was awesome. The day's caption was "Trust the Timing of Your Lessons" which read:

> "Too often our first inclination when we learn a lesson, gain a new insight, have an awareness, or glimpse a new truth; is to judge and criticize ourselves for not seeing it sooner, not knowing it before or being in total denial for too long. That is not necessary. It is not appropriate. We are not at fault because we did not have this awareness and understanding of this lesson until now. We don't need to see the truth one moment before we see it. Judging ourselves for not knowing sooner can close us off to what life has to teach us now. We are here to learn our lessons, discover our truths, have own adventures. Let yourself have your experiences. Allow yourself to learn what you learn when you learn it. Don't judge

> yourself for not learning sooner. Be happy, grateful and excited when your lesson arrives. Trust the timing of your heart."

How do I begin to talk about the awesomeness of God in our lives these past few weeks?

On Sunday the 20th of July 2008, my spirit led me to worship in Salvation Ministries Port-Harcourt which is located within GRA (Government Reserved Area) not far from my house. I was thrilled by the preaching of Pastor Ibiyeomie, the founder of the church, with his sermon titled "God is Everywhere". His opening line began thus:

> "It is not seeking forgiveness that brings forgiveness but seeking the Lord Jesus. One should seek the deliverer of miracles before one seeks for the miracle; for healing is everywhere. As recorded In Mathew Chapter 8, Jesus healed so many people in one day, and he healed them all. It is recorded that every time he saw the sick, compassion grew in him and their faith healed them and he always healed them all. He healed 2000 years ago and He still heals now."

The pastor laid emphasis on Jesus talking our infirmities away. He said "He took" several times saying that "took is took" and if he said He took, then He did because He would be made a liar and so if He took the infirmities then you do not have it any more.

He emphasized that faith is not for the future but is now. If it is not now then it is not faith. Jesus never told those who met him to come the next day. He took all the sickness, pain, cancer, liver diseases and so forth away. One should not dwell on the sickness, but look unto Jesus the healer because He took all infirmities away and so "took is took" for He simply took all infirmities away.

I was amazed at the crowd that worshipped at this ministry, but was particularly amazed by the flawless manner in which the ushers seated the congregation and the speed at which the seats were filled for the many services they held each Sunday.

I was disappointed at being unable to sit in the auditorium but a female usher told me sitting in the auditorium did not matter. What mattered was having faith for healing. She said my baby was too young to have faith so I should be the point of contact between the baby and the Lord Jesus, for through my faith, the baby could be healed.

I left at the end of the service feeling fulfilled and although we didn't have an instant miracle, I held on to my faith that Dike's tomorrow will be alright.

The Liver Report And The Third Dream

The next day, I took Dike and my office assistant Ivory who was ill, to see Dr. Ekeoku. There were so many people waiting to see him, but when I sent in Dike's medical report we were ushered in and attended to promptly. He took Dike's blood to sample for the liver functions and also took Ivory's blood for investigations. Afterwards, he wrote out a prescription for Dike who had nasal congestion and also prescribed malaria medication for Ivory. He asked us to pick up the results of the investigations the following day.

Ivory collected the medical reports the following day and when I studied Dike's, I was amazed to see a remarkable drop in his liver enzymes. The SGOT and SGPT were 18 IU/L and 14 IU/L respectively compare to the reading of 89 IU/L and 94 IU/L two weeks earlier (the normal range was 0-12I U/L).

The bilirubin was 122 U/moL/L direct, 99.4 u/moL/L for the conjugated while the alkaline phosphates was 63.4iu/L compared to 194 iu/L recorded two weeks earlier. I was stunned as I recalled the dream I had where the enzymes had decreased and was within the normal range.

I declared that Jesus was working out something great for Dike and He was giving me these signs to let me know He is the one in charge of our lives irrespective of the circumstances. My faith once more was lifted as I waited eagerly for the completion of the testimony in Dike life.

Close Of Business

As I made preparations to travel to the United States with the children, I decided to give up my office/shop in GRA Port-Harcourt. I asked my friend Chika if she would be interested in leasing the shop as my other friend Tarela, who had asked for it several times, was not ready to take the lease. After discussions with her husband, Chika took the lease for a two-year tenancy. My friend Kaine, who also had a shop like mine, bought some items from my shop. She was sad when she heard of Dike's ailment and our urgency to travel for a medical intervention, and wished us well. Later that week, Mike spoke to Dr. V.S.S. who advised us to continue all medications. Once again he said his diagnosis of Dike's ailment was certainly PFIC2.

CHAPTER 3

The Flying Dutchman

We should thank the Lord Almighty in every situation, for He knows and ordains every plan and journey of man. I have consistently seen the miracles of God in respect of our affairs especially in Dike's life, which enabled me to go on writing about his testimony.

I arrived Lagos with the children on Wednesday the 24th of July 2008 and we went to see Tonye in his office. He was so glad to see us and blessed us as we left him after our short stay in his office. His driver took us to spend the night with my friend Betty and her daughter Hephzibah.

The next day, we left for the USA with a stopover in Amsterdam. Just before we landed at Schipol Airport, a friendly airhostess asked me how the children and I were going to spend our transit time at the airport. I replied that we would hang around the airport till we boarded our connecting flight. She told me we could go sightseeing in Amsterdam by train from the airport and I was excited and grateful for the information. We disembarked and looked forward to a lovely adventure.

I called my cousin Chizoba and her husband who both worked with the Shell Petroleum Development Company (SPDC) on cross posting in the Netherlands. They were very excited to hear we were at the airport. They did not think we would be allowed into the city without the Schengen visas. Only two of my children had American passports which would enable them enter the Netherlands while the other two and myself had Nigerian passports. Okey advised we ask Immigrations if in doubt. We did and he was right so we had no choice but to wait in the airport. The children ran around playing with some other children who were also in transit with their parents.

After the long wait, our flight was cancelled and we were assigned to various hotels at the airport after some stipend was disbursed to each passenger. We did not have a change of clothes so I asked the ground staff of the airline if there was any chance of us being allowed to stay in a hotel outside the airport so we could shop for our basic needs. She was kind enough to talk to Immigration on our behalf but advised we make no mention of our having relatives in the city because they would not want to take a chance in keeping us out of their reach.

We were so grateful to this kind lady and as soon as the visas were issued, we called Okey and he came and picked us up. I told him about Dike's condition especially God's handwork in seeing us through to that moment. It was such a beautiful and impromptu family re–union and that became the glory of own summer vacation. In the early morning, Chizoba took me sightseeing; we went to The Hague and the Shell Headquarters. We later went to a pharmacy and I brought Vitamin K, Prednisolone and Questran which were some of the medications Dike needed but which I could not find in

Nigeria. We then headed back home to pick the children, and then we were off to the airport.

We arrived Dulles International Airport in Washington D.C on the 26th of July 2008 at 3.30pm. Cousin Dike came to pick us from the airport and we went home to meet his family of four. My sister-in-law, Vera who is a gynaecologist, visited us and we discussed Dike's condition. She gave me some documents on liver diseases to understand more about his condition.

After our first week on vacation, we went to Columbia city to spend some time with my cousin Rumundaka, his wife Chizoba and their three children. We exhausted Dike's medication Ondansetron, so my cousin Ada who is a medical doctor, took me to some pharmacies to see if we could get some. I was surprised to find that a 50 ml bottle of Ondansetron cost as much $350.00. We could not even purchase it without a prescription from a pediatrician. We also needed to get Simyl MCT oil which helps Dike with digestion. I blamed myself for my lack of foresight in not buying at least six months' supply of these medications while in India. I thought they could be found easily in most pharmacies. The different pharmacies visited checked the components of the MCT oil bottle and advised we try safflower oil or coconut oil. At Arundell Mill Mall, I saw a tin of edible coconut oil which cost $11.00 and believing it would be a good supplement for the MCT oil, I gladly bought it for Dike.

As a result of the difficulty encountered in getting the medication, I decided to ask Ken and Nathalie to help purchase them from India. My cousin Dike helped us send money and they got the prescription from Dr. V.S.S. which he endorsed as "lifesaving drugs" to enable the courier companies accept them. The MCT oil was not accepted into the USA by the courier as it was liquid but could be couriered to Nigeria, so I asked that it be sent there. The three months' supply of all the medication cost R7, 000.00 (Rupees.) The sum of $300.00 was sent which also covered shipping and handling with some change which we left to Ken and Nathalie for their logistics.

We had another challenge with Dike's diet. My cousin's wife Adaora Wonodi, a neonatologist, helped us purchase an infant formula for premature babies as she tried to get us a medical appointment to see some liver specialists. She advised that we do some blood tests while we awaited the appointment. It took 11 days to get the test results, which was unusual. It kept us in suspense and was also a point of stress for me. We had also given samples for some vitamin tests which we felt was unnecessary and expensive; moreover we never got to see that report.

On the 8th of August 2008, Adaora came to see us with her daughter Oma, who is also my god- daughter. When she left, she took all Dike's medical reports for a review in her workplace at John Hopkins Hospital.

Our vacation was going well. We had a 3-day family reunion to celebrate the birthdays of Dike and Yetunde's daughters Urenna and Onaedo, as well as their christening. It was the best part of our vacation as we bonded with family and friends.

As I read the Open Heavens devotional for 10th of August 2008 titled "Not Forsaken" which detailed the healing at "The Beautiful Gate" with the text taken from the Book of Acts 3: 1-11; once again I saw a ministration concerning Dike's condition. It held that every problem in your life has an expiry date; God's plan is to bring the best out of your worst. Between the manufacture date and the expiration date of a problem, you should stay in the place of faith and look up to God. As you look up in faith and continue to serve, worship and praise Him, irrespective of your challenges, the problem could expire before its programmed date. I studied these scriptures,

"There is a season for everything"
Ecclesiastes 3: 1-2

This was the word I needed to key into.

Dike's medications finally arrived in the USA through DHL on the 11th of August 2008. We were required to send some information such as the generic names of the medication, the dosage, the quantities ordered, the doctor's prescription, a USA resident's social security number, and an endorsement by the resident as the importer of the medication, before they could be released to us. I was made to understand this was standard protocol and we had to wait a few days for the medication to be released.

In the course of this bureaucracy, we ran out of Ondansetron by Monday the 11th and two days later, Dike started vomiting. I became very worried and on Saturday, I called Adaora who prescribed Benadryl anti-histamine. He vomited once after taking the medication but then the vomiting stopped and I became relieved. Chizoba bought Paedialyte for him to replenish his electrolytes as he had become so dehydrated. Dike's body had become so itchy he could hardly managed to take his other medication. The Paedialyte made him feel better and we were able to visit Adaora's family to celebrate her second daughter Orukanwa's birthday.

We went to church on Sunday and Dike vomited again. We later went to Zim and Vera's house for another family gathering and Dike vomited yet again. I was now very worried. I eventually broke down in tears especially when one of my sisters-in-law made a statement insinuating that my concern about the cost of getting Dike's medication from a pharmacy within the USA was ill founded. She gave the impression that I was being irrational by not prioritizing

Dike's medication. I was so upset with her unkind words because she had no idea of our ordeal with Dike's health and his well-being, nor what I was going through at that time with the sleepless nights, the constant feeding and stooling, and most especially the severe anxiety caused by the delay in the delivery of his medication. She probably thought that I did not buy the medication because it was expensive but in truth we needed a doctor's prescription from an approved source for it to be dispensed. We had at least seven practicing medical doctors in our family yet it was not easy to get the prescription. Adaora had tried to schedule an appointment with a liver doctor and was able to get us a one-hour appointment in Georgetown University Hospital, Washington D.C and that process took a whole month.

I wept so bitterly. Seeing how desperate the situation had become, Vera who is a practicing gynaecologist, called various pharmacies to order the medication but the pharmacists refused to fill in the prescription. When she explained that she is a gynaecologist and was recommending the medication for her patient who was vomiting, the pharmacists recommended another brand of the medication which was much cheaper. She had a tough time convincing each pharmacist that she wanted Ondansetron for her patient. After several phone calls and very long talks, one pharmacist finally agreed to dispense the medication. She told me the pharmacy will probably call me later to get details and maybe try to talk me into settling for some cheaper medication since they just did not understand why I would pay so much more for a medication that had a cheaper alternative.

We got back late that evening and Anyi went to pick up the medication after the pharmacy C.V.S called. It cost $70.00 for 4 tablets and on that Sunday the 17th of August, at 11.30pm Dike finally took the medication. We were so relieved from the six days of severe itching. Two hours later when I had to give him the routine medication, I mistakenly gave him another tablet of Ondansetron but did not realise my mistake until about thirty minutes later. I had been so exhausted from the day and was almost asleep on my feet and I began to fret and shake, feeling confused. I tried to call Chizoba and Anyi for advice but they were also totally worn out. I was so worried but then remembered I could still pray. So I knelt down and prayed deeply and fervently; peace engulfed me. I became convinced that the second dose will not cause him any harm but instead would help relieve him much faster since he had been through so much itching and vomiting over the past few days. I fed him and he ate well, then slept so soundly into the morning.

On Monday morning, I wrote a compassionate letter to Alicia Hamette, the lady who had called me from her office regarding Dike's medication. I was not sure where the medication was at that point but prayed the medication would reach us before Dike finished the four tablets we had bought.

To my utmost dismay, my letter was not acknowledged and I received no reply. On Tuesday night, I received an e-mail from Ken in India who said he realised we were yet to receive the medications. He called the DHL office in Chennai and they confirmed I had not received the medication. They promised to talk to their USA office to speed up the delivery. I was not impressed by the DHL U.S. office's lack of communication and total suspense. I forwarded all my correspondence to justify the effort and it was more annoying knowing we were receiving information from India rather than the U.S. Office that was in possession of the medication.

On Thursday morning, Dike took the last tablet of Ondansetron and there was still no package from DHL. My brother Emmanuel visited us with his mother and his youngest daughter Petra all the way from New Jersey. We were in high spirits and he blew balloons for the children who were so fascinated by the large bubbles he blew. We took pictures and as they departed; Mum gave us $200 while Emmanuel gave $100.

Just before they left, I received an e-mail informing me Dike's medication had finally been cleared and would be delivered that Thursday. I was advised to call Mary on a certain number which I did immediately and she asked for the airway bill no. When I mistakenly dropped the phone to get this information the line cut and I could not reach her again after several attempts. It was so frustrating. Unfortunately, the medications were not delivered and I wondered if we could get some refill from CVS.

Later that day, Adaora called to inform me her team believed Dike had biliary atresia. She had scheduled an appointment for Tuesday at the Georgetown University and it would cost us about $500.00 to see the liver specialists.

On Sunday we went to Vera and Zim's house. I had to drive halfway to meet my cousin Dike and Yetunde, who would come from the opposite direction. Dike would then take over my car and drive the rest of the way. He would later drive us back to Rumundaka's with his wife driving behind us. It was a very busy period for them all and that option was the only feasible solution to enable us have a day out. It was also a brilliant arrangement which boosted my confidence in driving in the United States.

One evening during the last week of our vacation, Dike Ibe came to Columbia to take us to Gettysburg so we could stay in the Wyndham Hotel and be closer to the shopping district. That particular day, I was very anxious and weepy with all the saddled challenges ahead of me. We had just a few more days in the USA. I walked into the hotel feeling so downcast despite its ambience which reminded us of the Protea Hotel where we spent Christmas and New Year prior to Dike's delivery. We walked into the room with a beautifully laid king-sized bed and a lot of throw pillows with the middle one in the shape of a sweet wrap with a monogram which read "BE WELL". I was awed by that welcome and I knew that all would be well. This again became another confirmation concerning Dike's healing.

At midday on Friday, Yetunde took us shopping at IKEA to buy some items for our new home in Abuja. On our way Chizoba called to inform me that Dike's medications had been delivered and I thanked God. The night before, Dike Senior had gone and bought four more tables for Dike Junior and I was grateful that he and Anyi asked me not to pay back the money they spent. I was already feeling relieved that I had four new tablets for a few days when the news of the delivery got to me.

The Open Heavens message for Monday, 18th of August 2008 was titled "It Will Be Worse" with the text taken from 1 John 2: 15–17. This was a pointer to what we were going through waiting for Dike's medication. The medication had actually arrived from the United States on the 11th of August 2008 but seven days later, when I read the devotional I was speechless. The commentary stated "If Jesus is your healer, then there will be no cause for alarm even when the most basic drug is out of circulation".

I read the devotional for Saturday, 23rd of August 2008 titled "Any Dividends of Worship", where the commentary held that our attitude towards worship can determine success or failure in our lives. Noah's worship brought great dividends for the entire human race. Any victory not sandwiched between worship can be touched by the kingdom of darkness. If our victory, success or breakthrough is at the verge of being stolen or lost, we need to examine ourselves. I quickly reminded myself that my brother Tonye gave testimonies every time God did something significant for him. This ministered to me concerning our plight with Dike, so I asked God to make me a true worshipper as advised by the action point for the day.

On Tuesday the 26th of August 2008, Ada came to the hotel and picked us up to go for the appointment with the liver specialists at Georgetown University Hospital in Washington D.C.

We met with the paediatric liver specialists and they said they were convinced Dike had biliary atresia. He weighed about 14Lbs/6.4kg and was almost 8 months old. In the past 4 months, his growth had become stunted. He had also lost a lot of weight as a result of the frequent stooling, dehydration and the vomiting of the past weeks. I noticed a lot of change in him though he still looked very handsome. The doctor who was the liver specialist said although Dike looked okay, we should be aware that any little ailment would threaten his life for his G.G.T, which she pointed out, was over 499.

While in India, Dike's GGT was 35 and this was one of the factors Dr. V.S.S. considered in his diagnosis which made him conclude Dike had PFIC 2 and not biliary atresia. During our consultation, the doctor asked who a likely donor would be for a liver transplant. Ada and I told her the father had the match but was worried about the consequences of donating. They assured us that in their practice, they would never take an organ from an unwilling person even if that person later changed his mind, as a result of the very high risk of litigation especially in the U.S., a fact we clearly understood.

The conclusion after their consultation was it did not matter anymore what the issue with Dike was, because the solution to any of the issues would still be a liver transplant unless God gave us a miracle. Ada and I had been told the doctor's opinion and we were running out of time. We were told that if there was ever a child that was diagnosed with biliary atresia and had turned two years old then the ailment would certainly not be biliary atresia; most did not even live to see their first birthday.

We left Georgetown University Hospital with my heart in my mouth. I was downcast and begged God to give me the grace to face what lay ahead of us. I was not going to let my handsome boy go without putting up a fight to save him. God had given me such good omens to enable me once more reject the doctor's report.

Ada took us to the White House and that was when President Barak Obama had just been voted into office but had not yet been sworn in. Ada sat in her car, while the children and I walked down to the tourist section of the White House to take some photographs. I did not know what the future held for Dike but I just wanted our visit to the USA to be a memorable vacation for the children. I continued with my writings having the justification that the revelation to write down as much as I could of the prophecies, messages and divine encounters I had meant that God was not asleep concerning what seemed like a hopeless situation.

Ada took us back to the hotel after a quick stop at Wal-Mart. Yetunde later came by and took us to her house so I could take their car to drive around the next day. My cousin Dike worked in Chicago during the week and came home every weekend. Yetunde on the other hand, had just resumed work after her maternity leave and had two little children to take care of without a nanny. It was easier for us to stay close to the shopping district and have the car so I would not depend on them for everything. We only had a few more days stay in the US and needed to do our back-to-school shopping and also get some more things for the new house in Abuja.

A few weeks back, while at Rumundaka and Chizoba's house in Colombia, Chizoba and I had discussed Dike's medical challenge and the plight I found myself in. I had told her I would not mind donating my liver to save any of my loved ones. We concluded that the doctors might want to try to use my liver to save someone else if the other recipient has a family member who would have a match for Dike. Chizo's suggestion was a figment of our imagination we wished would be possible.

There are times when dreams appear unrealistic but nothing should stop us from dreaming, for dreams are a part of reality and we often do not know what is realisable till we begin to dream.

Sometimes we just need a little imagination to discover things are not as impossible as we believe. I had come back from the hospital with some brochures and documents on liver transplant which I was asked to study. I was also given the cost of a transplant procedure in the USA. It would cost about $450,000 (four hundred and fifty thousand dollars) for a foreigner who had no health insurance cover and this was just for the period of stay in hospital.

That was a lot of money and the chance of getting a liver through the liver transplant register was impossible since we were not even American citizens. The sad reality still remained as the doctors told us, that most people on a waiting list do not live long enough to receive a liver.

The only consolation I had was a phone call from Rumundaka that evening. He had called to ask how the doctor's appointment went and I told him what had transpired in a very weepy voice. To my surprise, Rumundaka said I should wipe away my tears that Dike is worth his giving a part of his liver to and said he would go to his doctor the next day to find out his blood group. He knew it had a

B but was not sure if it was AB or B, and was also not sure if it was positive or negative. He assured me that as we live in the 21st century, he has always been open to medial advancements and technological breakthroughs because he benefits from them, especially with his family.

My cousin also told me that his wife's father had died young of liver cancer which left his mother-in-law with the great responsibility of raising her many children alone; his wife, Chizoba, being the eldest. Reminiscing on these facts, he said to me that he would not sit and watch his nephew's life be snuffed out because he wanted to hoard his own liver. He told me he would discuss with his wife and then discuss his insurance package and his fitness to donate with his doctor and get back to me.

Rumundaka's words were like a breath of fresh air to my downcast life. It was all I needed to hear at that point and whether he would later give his liver or not did not matter. All I needed was that reassurance that someone was willing to save Dike and was going to make an effort to do so, thereby reassuring me that I was not alone in the struggle. I was thrilled for it had always been said that help usually comes from the most unlikely quarters. Yetunde was with us at the Wyndham hotel when I had this conversation with my cousin.

I talked with Ada later and she told me to keep away my fears and focus on getting the kids back to school and on furnishing my new home in Abuja. I was so exhausted and I asked God to give me the strength to bear this issue and give Dike the grace not to suffer. I went to bed at about 1.40am.

On Thursday the 28th of August 2008, Yetunde took us to Rumundaka's new home in Ellicott City. We did our last bit of shopping the next day as our vacation had finally come to an end.

Our departure was on a very rainy day and there was so much traffic on the highway. I prayed we would not miss our flight. The journey took two hours in the rain and by the time we got to the airport, Ada had been waiting for about an hour with some of our luggage which she had picked up from Yetunde and Dike's home.

While in traffic. Rumundaka received a call from his doctor with results of his blood test. He was not a match for our son Dike. My heart went out to my cousin, and I acknowledged he had become my hero and would always remain a brother.

We got to the airport in the nick of time to check in. All the suitcases Ada had brought were overweight and we did not have the time to repack them. Rumundaka paid the excess baggage charge with the money he had planned to give us, which was very kind of him. We were probably the last of the passengers to check in and we proceed to board the aircraft immediately.

Mike was waiting for us when we arrived Nigeria. It was really good to see him and the children were so excited to see their father again. We spent the night in Lagos at the Knightbridge Hotel, which is owned by my cousin Obinna. The next day, we all excitedly flew into Abuja at noon to begin a new life in the beautiful capital city Abuja.

Settling Down In Abuja

We stayed in my Aunt May's residence for a while. We immediately settled Ugonna into the Nigerian Turkish International School where she had gained admission for the first year of her Junior Secondary School. Amaka and Dalu were enrolled into The Lead British International School, reputed to be a good school in our neighbourhood.

On Sunday the 7th of September 2008, Dike turned 8 months. Pat Ozigbo, my friend and neighbour in Port Harcourt, came to Abuja with her two daughters Eki and Naame. Eki had already done her first year at the Nigerian Turkish International School and Naame was going into her first year with my daughter Ugonna; they had both taken the entrance examination together. Pat had already dropped her daughters off in school before coming to stay with us at my Aunt's home.

While with us, she convinced me to cut Dike's hair which had grown very long. During our vacation in the United States, I had used rubber bands to hold his hair in balls like a girl's and he looked very much like his sister Dalu.

Mike had gone back to Port Harcourt soon after we arrived Abuja. He needed to tend to his mother who had been ill while we were away on vacation. She had stayed in her daughter's house in Port-Harcourt, and had suffered a loss of appetite and fatigue. She collapsed and was immediately taken to our family doctor at Anchor Hospital. Mama eventually got better and was discharged, so Mike took her back to our own home in Port-Harcourt. Mike had brought Reverend Hart from Christ Church Port-Harcourt to pray for her; she gradually got better and started eating again as the days progressed.

This ailment, however, became a turning point in Mama's life for she was seventy-nine years old and diabetic. Her outlook on life had changed when she turned seventy, when it seemed as if the reality of old age had set in. Her health began to decline and we did all we could to give her a very comfortable life for which she was very appreciative. I often took her to see various specialists for her medical check-ups. I loved her so much; she was kind hearted and often told me that the day she would pass on she would do it so peacefully and would not even lock the door so we would reach her without having to break the door down.

Our friends in India called to say they had gone to see Dr. V.S.S. who advised we stop all medication except Udiliv, Reneliv and Complete T.D. I stopped the medication as advised, but Dike vomited that evening. I gave him Vomikind, which is another brand of Ondansetron, and he vomited again. I waited for some hours before giving it to him a second time and eventually, the vomiting stopped.

I spoke to Dr. V.S.S. and he advised I gave M.C.T oil. I later made arrangements for Dike Ibe to send about $300 to Ken and Nathalie to enable us order more medication and feeds from India since it was easy to send money to India from the United States and almost impossible then from Nigeria.

I called Ugonna in school and also visited her within the week. I was glad she liked her new school and had settled in easily. I was grateful to God for that so I could focus on settling the other children, attending to Dike and settling into the new house.

The Everlasting Covenant Parish Of The Redeemed Christian Church Of God

I spoke to Mike early on Sunday the 14th of September 2008 and he asked after our well-being and if I was planning to go to church. I told him I did not plan to go to church and he suggested I go with the children to the Redeem Christian Church of God opposite my aunt's house, rather than just stay at home. I was glad he suggested this because I did not know where to go with the children and I was not in the mood to go to an Anglican church for a long day of worship. With Dike's condition of constant feeding and diaper changing, coupled with his heavy sweating in a hot city like Abuja, I needed to keep him indoors most times.

After our conversation, I got the children ready and we all went to the church. It was a wonderful service. When the testimony time was announced, I came out to join the testifiers and presented Dike to the church. I was awed by my utterances for what I had planned to say eluded me and I ended up presenting baby Dike to them for prayers, emphatically stating that "It is well".

When I gave my testimony about Dike it seemed that the heavens opened. The pastors rose to their feet and asked me to lay Dike at the altar; they prayed fervently for him after which I picked him up and went back to my seat.

As I sat down, an usher, Brother Lekan, sent me a note asking that I join him in a three-day fast for Dike's health. I was amazed at his faith and care for a child he did not know. Shortly afterwards, I received another note from the choir director, Pastor Faith, asking me to "bring Dike to the choir at the end of the service so he could sing to the Lord".

At the end of the service, the Pastor-in- Charge of the parish, Pastor Alaye Tokubie Ogan, and the other pastors and elders of the church prayed again for Dike. The pastor told us all that he was impressed by my testimony especially my boldness in presenting the baby to the Lord and my emphasis that "It is well". He likened this to the story of the Shunammite woman who said "It is well" to the prophet of God even when her son had just died (2 Kings 4: 23-27). I knew that it was God who gave me the words for my testimony rather than what I had composed in my head.

After the short session with the pastor, I took Dike to the choir and the choristers prayed and laid hands on him. Pastor Faith told me to bring Dike to the choir any time I worshipped in the parish so Dike would sing to the Lord. He said he would appoint someone to carry him during the service if I did not want to sit with the choir.

Before we left, the multi-talented keyboardist, who also plays the guitar and drums, came to me and said he would teach Dike to play the musical instruments.

I was so touched by the outpouring of love in the church and I knew in my heart that God had directed me to worship at that parish on that special day.

It is important to note that God can give a command or a direction through a vessel but the choice remains ours to heed the instruction. My husband Mike was the vessel that morning and I had the choice to go or not to go to the church. I was glad that I had made up my mind to go and we arrived as the second service was about to begin, just in time for the testimonies session which usually comes after the praise and worship.

This encounter with the church became a turning point for us; it was the anchor for our faith and salvation all through our journey into the unknown. We knew all would be well eventually, although the going would not be easy.

After the service, I met with the wives of the two pastors, Dr. Mrs. Evelyn Ogan and Mrs. Ada Aki. Their warmth and friendliness overwhelmed me. Our daughter Amaka was also very excited and told me she wished we would continue our worship at the parish. I was very glad the children felt the same way I did about the parish.

I invited Pastor Ogan to come over to our new house to dedicate it since we were meant to move in on that day. He instructed three members of the prayer/pastoral group to go with me and he promised to visit our home the next Sunday as he already had several meetings lined up after the service. They went with me to the house, prayed and anointed the front gate, exterior grounds and walls before I took them back to church.

We lived in our Abuja home for four and a half years and remained grateful to God for His protection throughout our stay in that house. We would later understand that our street was frequently besieged by armed robbers for a few years before we moved in. We did not relent in our prayer life and the Lord kept us safe from harm. For two years, we had relative peace on that street until we began to hear the horrifying stories that the robbers had started their operations once more.

The night I heard my neighbour's scream as they were being attacked by armed robbers, was the most horrifying night I had ever experienced. But the Lord delivered our neighbour that night. After that incident, the residents of our street had series of meetings about securing the street and we communicated with the area police command. The police began patrolling our neighbourhood every night from then on.

We would often call the mobile police units in our district whenever we heard any disturbing noise late at night. We also had to install a porter-cabin as a security post behind our street, which was near the major highway, as this was where the criminals came through to attack the houses. With all the measures we put in place, we finally had some peace during the last one year we lived there. I believe our prayers outside the gate and the anointing of our premises on that first day before we took up the occupancy, kept evil away from us. Our compound was not as secured as we would have wanted, considering that our gateman was not equipped as a security man and our doors were simply made of wood and not bullet proof. Our sufficiency was simply of God, for if the robbers were to invade our home, only the grace of God would have delivered us.

I met a lady called Ego Offorjindu at the children's new school the week before their resumption, when I went to pick up their school uniforms. She had also come to pick up school uniforms for her three-year old son, Omasiri. She introduced herself and told me she worked in a construction company in the Gwarimpa Estate where we lived.

During our conversation, I told her I needed an electrician to help with some electrical installations in our home and she immediately recommended one. She later became a close friend and was of tremendous help all through our stay in Abuja; I had no doubt God brought her my way when we met. She would later bring me a plumber and a carpenter to help me put finishing touches to the house.

On Monday the 15th of September 2008, Dalu and Amaka resumed classes at the Lead British International which is a two-minute drive from the house; it was an exciting day for all of us.

On Wednesday the 17th September, I received a text message from Aniete, a brother who is a member of the church choir. It read thus:

> "Unto us a son is given, his name is called Dike. By him we shall not only be heard of but be seen and felt by this generation. Just give God praise for his gift. Know that Hezekiah got God by asking 'Can the dead praise you?' Dike, a great psalmist has nothing to do with what the doctor said."

I was so touched by Aniete's message and I gave glory to God once more for surrounding us with people who truly cared for us.

I was most often touched when people found time out of their schedules to call and pray for us. Those were the momentum I needed to forge ahead during those challenging times.

Flash back to the 18th of August 2008. My brother Bay, called me from the United States. He said that he had just heard about Dike's health and had called to pray with us. We had not been able to talk during our vacation in the United States a few months earlier. Another friend, Suzie Asa, also called from Port-Harcourt with a similar burden in her heart, having last seen us the day we left Port Harcourt. Then my sister in-law, Nona, called from Port Harcourt where she had gone to visit my ailing mother-in-law and my husband Mike. She was so weepy on the phone and I was so touched by her care and emotions. I considered myself blessed to be surrounded by such prayer warriors. My family and friends were so amazing and I knew in my heart that God would hear and grant our collective request to heal Dike.

Meanwhile, on Wednesday the 17th of September 2008, while at Dalu's tea party in her school, I received a call from my close friend Aunty Tonia Diai whom I chose as the Godmother to our first child, Ugonna. She had relocated to South Africa and was in Nigeria visiting friends in Abuja and had also planned to see us.

She visited us at home on Sunday the 21st of September 2008 and we had a hearty conversation sharing testimonies of what the Lord had done for us. She told me she was now a full time pastor in South Africa and shared a revelation she had about ten years back. She said she saw a toddler with a bulging stomach who was given to her for prayers. The child and people were watching to see what would happen as she prayed. The child died and the people began to leave when it became obvious there was nothing else they could do to save him. After a while, the body of the child began to decompose but she continued to pray and a few people who had stayed behind began to mock her. But then she saw the baby stir! She intensified her prayers and suddenly the child came back to life. The baby passed some stool which rid the body of all its toxins, and his stomach collapsed to a normal sized one. What an interesting revelation!

Aunty Tonia and I had lost touch for a few years and she did not know what we had gone through with Dike's health, so seeing this condition grieved her heart. She knelt and asked God Almighty to deliver Dike whom she likened to the child in the revelation she had ten years earlier. We reaffirmed and acknowledged that Dike's condition was not unto death but for the Lord Jesus to be glorified.

Our SOS Call

The Open Heaven devotional for Saturday 20th of September 2008 was "SOS Call" and the text was taken from Psalm 27:3.

> "Though a host should encamp against me, my heart shall not fear: though war should rise against me, in this will I be confident."
> Psalm 27:3

The devotional held that problems are potential testimonies and the bigger they are the greater the testimonies. When God is about to do something great, He looks out for big problems to use as raw materials; and to perform a miracle; He usually starts with the impossible. The action point read, "Are you in an emergency? Send an S.O.S. message to Heaven today".

That day, while in church for choir practice, I suddenly realised that Dike's cereal was almost finished and we only had one tin of Elementum and one tin of Dexolac left. I didn't know what to do and

I asked the Lord for direction. I blamed myself for not taking stock earlier and placing an order through our Indian friends. Then I remembered that when I had stopped by my aunt May's house earlier that evening, she had mentioned that her sister, Dr. Nwosu had made a stop-over in Dubai on her way to India. She had not spoken to her and did not have a contact number for her yet. I had to send an SOS to God.

I had not thought of it when she mentioned this to me while we dined at her home, and it did not occur to me that this was an opportunity presenting itself for Dike's need. As I got home and took proper stock of his feeds and medication, I became worried at the short supply left. Then I remembered the information my aunt gave me earlier that evening! I called my aunt's daughter in Lagos asking for her mother's contact number, but she did not have it yet; I spent the night anticipating her call so we could tell her our need.

We went to church on Sunday; it was a bright and sunny day. Pastor Faith took Dike from me and carried him all through the praise and worship session, afterwards he handed Dike over to the senior parish Pastor, Alaye Ogan who carried him all through the sermon.

I was pleasantly surprised as the sermon for the day was specially prepared for Dike and was a declaration of thanksgiving for "our little brother Dike" as the Pastor called him. As he preached, he said that whatever the doctors said or called the ailment he had, it did not matter. His reference for this declaration was Matthew 11: 28-30.

> "Come unto me all ye that labor and are heavy laden and I will give you rest. Take my yoke upon you and learn of me; for I am meek and lowly in heart: and ye

shall find rest unto your souls; for my yoke is easy and my burden is light."
Matthew 11: 28-30

After the congregation celebrated Dike in prayers and thanksgiving, some of us expected the main sermon to be delivered but to our surprise, the offerings and tithes were collected and the service came to a close. This act of brotherhood humbled and amazed me as I realised that Dike was the caption for the day. The sermon was simply the celebration of Dike and not even prayers to save Dike.

The Everlasting Covenant Parish of the Redeemed Christian Church of God was a totally different experience and my guests Chinelo Onyekesi and her children, were also very touched by the Pastor's ministration; she advised me to keep attending that parish and if possible become an active member for it was obvious we had found a home there.

After the service, Dike remained the toast of everyone. We eventually went home and celebrated our Sunday with a sumptuous lunch of fried rice, coleslaw, chicken stew and fried plantain – our favourite. Once again, we praised the Lord for His faithfulness in our lives.

At midnight, I received a call from my Aunt May that my aunt Dr. Nwosu had just called her so she gave me her contact number. I called her at once as she was already boarding the flight to Mumbai. She asked me to send her a text message detailing what we needed and I did just that. It was an answered prayer for the SOS concerning Dike's need.

With all the daily revelations I received, and the grace I had to see spiritually and to understand and appreciate them all, I had no doubt that the story I was documenting was to strengthen people's faith. I believed in the serendipity of God which is the unmerited grace He gives to His children of which I am a benefactor.

I spent the next three days to pray and fast for Dike. I usually stayed up from midnight to dawn to pray, read and write.

Your New Era Starts Now

The Message in the Open Heavens Devotional of Monday 22nd September 2008 was titled Your New Era Starts Now with text taken from Genesis 1:1-4. A New Era is the beginning of a divine programme which closes the chapter of Satan's imprints, handwritings and manipulations.

On Tuesday the 23rd of September 2008, I went to the Lead British for Dalu's Assembly and was thrilled when she was recognized and given a certificate as the most caring pupil in her class. I thanked God once more for the all-around blessings the Lord had given my children.

Later in the day, I went with my new friend Ego to inspect one of her sites: As an Estate Management professional, she was also a property developer. While we inspected her project, I received a call from Port Harcourt. It was Elizabeth, the lady who brought Blessing, Dike's nanny, to us. She asked that Blessing be released to come home to attend to one of their aunties who had fallen ill. I immediately became fainthearted for I knew a major challenge was brewing for me and my household. We needed the extra help.

As I thought about what to do, I recalled the Bible passage from Pastor Ogan's message taken from Matthew 11:28-30.

> "Come unto me all ye that labor and are heavy laden and I will give you rest. Take my yoke upon you and learn of me for I am meek and lowly in heart and ye shall find rest unto your souls, for my yoke is easy and my burden is light."
> Matthew 11:28-30

I meditated upon this passage for the rest of the day and knew I would need to have a word with Blessing. As I pondered on the challenge that lay ahead, I was apprehensive as I needed some help with the children, especially as Dike needed a little more care than the others.

Although I was faced with the challenge of Blessing leaving us and returning to her people, I took it in good faith. She was such a good girl, very truthful and hardworking but I said to myself, if she had to leave, then go she will.

I continued to read the Open Heavens devotional daily, believing there was always a message that would minister to my heart. I remember the teaching on the ways to deal with the challenges or "mountains" in our lives. The memory verse ministered to me as I felt in my heart that God would strengthen me for the challenge ahead.

> "But they that wait upon the Lord shall renew their strength. They shall mount up with wings as eagles; they shall run and not be weary and they shall run and not faint."
> Isaiah 40: 31

Later that night, I finally had a discussion with Dike's nanny Blessing, and we agreed she would leave on Sunday morning. She wept all through the remaining days she spent with us and I was also heartbroken for she came into our family on the 7th of January 2008, the day Dike was born and for the first time in my marriage, I had a stress free domestic life. Blessing in turn was weepy and very upset with her people because for the first time in her life, she was with a family that took her in as one of theirs. She was convinced her people did not care about her progress and was certain her aunt was being mischievous in asking her to come back to attend to an ailing aunt whom she did not think existed.

The Open Heavens message for that day, the 26th of September 2008 was titled "Managing Distractions" with the text taken from Matthew 14: 24–33. The prayer in the devotional message for the day was "Father, help me to shut my eyes and ears to every distraction and focus on you until I reach my goal". I looked to the Lord for help to get a replacement for Blessing; a good nanny was very difficult to come by.

The message for Saturday the 27th of September was titled "Fear Forbidden" with the text from Isaiah 43: 1–3. The message stated that it is foolhardy to look up to someone who cannot help you in time of trouble. Those who have confidence in man in times of trouble are under a curse. Elisha spontaneously told his servant to fear not, and the Bible has about 365 "fear nots" which gives an average dose of one "fear not" per day. This was very thought provoking.

I dropped Blessing off at the motor park early morning on Sunday as planned, then went to church with the children. After the service the Senior Pastors came home with us to bless and anoint our home.

They particularly prayed to the Lord to make the house uncomfortable for anyone who was not meant to be there.

The next day, our rather lazy security man informed me he was leaving. I was so excited and convinced it was the Holy Spirit that made him leave, for I had been planning to fire him as he was not worth keeping.

The message in the Open Heavens that Monday the 29th of September 2008 was titled “A New Chapter” with text taken from Exodus 12: 2–12. It urged us not to lose hope for the Lord was introducing a new chapter into our lives which would turn our sorrows into joy and our weeping into celebration.

After the midweek service on Tuesday, I mentioned to Pastor Ogan that our security man had left. He immediately called Ezekiel the church security man, to bring his brother James who was with him, to come work for us. James went with us to start work as our security man but informed us he would have to stop work in December for personal reasons. We agreed to this and did not mind at all.

Pastor Ogan introduced us to Gideon who was a brother in church. He told Gideon to take charge of all the electrical issues we had at home; he was an experienced electrician working with the Julius Berger construction company. I was very touched by Pastor Ogan’s fatherly gestures. I had not told him about the numerous electrical, carpentry and plumbing challenges we had in the house. Our house looked beautiful in and out but on closer inspection, the finishing was very poor and it was expensive to maintain.

I was very sceptical about bringing artisans into my home as they are often know to be insincere and sometimes initiate theft in homes in collusion with the domestic staff. I was grateful that Pastor Ogan stepped in to address some of the pressing issues we had.

The medication and formula my cousin Dike Senior paid for finally arrived. However, I was rather upset when the TNT courier representative called and asked that I pay a certain amount of money into a private account to enable them pay off the customs service before we could receive them. He advised me to pay or else we would not receive the package at all. I remembered what we went through with the DHL and FDA in the USA and reluctantly complied; Dike was on the last tin of formula and I needed the package delivered urgently. I paid the said amount and the package of Dike's feed was dispatched to me. When the courier handler handed the package over to me, he also demanded some money for the delivery and in my anger, I told him off as there was no justification for that demand.

Interestingly, my brother Tonye had visited us the day before and we spent some time discussing a few pertinent issues. He talked about bribery and corruption, and was of the opinion that when people fail to plan ahead, they usually fall victim to those who extort. In other words, the bribe givers are often those who are desperate having failed to plan ahead. The remedy therefore is to be patient, plan ahead and be ready to do a lot of talking and negotiating.

What Tonye said made a lot of sense, however in the country we live in, even if one planned ahead, these issues would most often still rear their ugly heads every now and then. We all needed God's intervention in our daily affairs.

When I mailed Ken and Nathalie to acknowledge receipt of the package and told them of the money I paid before it was released to me, they took action and forwarded my e-mail to the TNT office in Chennai, who in turn forwarded the e-mail to their Lagos office. I was surprised when the Lagos office called me to find out what had transpired, but I told them I did not want to discuss it further for I did not want to open a can of worms which would likely get someone fired. I felt the documented evidence they had was enough and they could put checks in place to avoid a future occurrence if they wanted to.

Knowing that I would most likely require their services in the near future, as they seemed to be the only courier company that would deliver the formula and the medication from Chennai, I decided not to expose the defaulting staff for he could go out to frustrate my next order.

Ever since Dr. V.S.S. had asked us to stop most of Dike's medication, I noticed that he had begun to gradually react adversely to the ailment that besieged him. His stooling had become more frequent, his body had begun to itch again and his skin was becoming very dry; he was also very dehydrated. I needed a good paediatrician to examine him urgently as his discomfort grew. Pastor Eke and his wife Ada Aki recommended their family doctor at Zanklee Hospital in the Utako area of Abuja. It took me a while to locate the hospital as we were still new in the city.

The paediatrician was not in the office and the attending general practitioner was yet to arrive at the hospital. As I did not feel comfortable seeing a general practitioner, we went back home.

I later received a call from Dr. Gbogbo the paediatric surgeon in Port –Harcourt. He wanted an update on Dike and I briefed him on the USA liver specialists' opinion at the Georgetown University Hospital. He said it did not matter what the doctor said for PFIC and biliary atresia were the same to him because both ailments had the same solution, which was a liver transplant. He said that even after the liver transplant is successfully achieved, the management of the child will not be easy and would require frequent travels for his medical check-up.

Mummy Meg

In the early morning of Wednesday, the 1st of October 2008, the Nigerian Independence Day, I called my bosom friend, Chi-Chi's mum, whom I fondly call Mummy Meg. Mummy Meg has always bridged the gap since the loss of my mother as a child. She was very compassionate, loving and always celebrated with me on my special occasions - from all my birthdays in my four years in the university, my graduation, my marriage, coming to nurse me at the birth of my children (the *omugwo* as it is known in our Igbo culture), to calling every member of my family on our birthdays.

While we were in the USA, she was in London on vacation and we had spoken several times. I did not call her again after we left Germantown to the District of Columbia and this upset her very much. She said she had made repeated calls to the number she had but did not get a response. She scolded me for my misconduct but mostly for making her so worried by not allowing her share in my challenge with Dike's health. She accused me of hiding facts from her and always having reservations rather than opening up to her. I apologized and made up with her.

Mummy Meg wanted an update on Dike and I briefed her on the situation. She shocked me when she said she would donate her liver to save her grandson, after all she had done all she had to do in the world and if saving Dike would mean the end of her life then so be it. I was so amazed to hear this and I knew there could be no greater love than Mummy's love and sacrifice for her family. She said she would immediately make an appointment with her doctor in London and brief me on their decision after her blood and liver tests.

I was humbled by her heart of love but deep down I knew she could not donate her liver, for she was over seventy years old and the doctors would not take an organ from a donor who was over fifty-five years.

After we spoke, I became euphoric, knowing that help was on its way and I remained cheerful for a while until the reality of Dike's condition manifested once more.

We stayed home that Independence Day and I plaited my daughters' hair. Later in the day, I received a message from Tonye, urging that we fast and pray for the growth of his house fellowship. I told him I would join in the Thursday fast and would also use the opportunity to believe God for a fellowship centre for our Everlasting Covenant Parish at my home.

Later that day, Brother Gideon came over to do some electrical work for us. He was sympathetic about Dike's case and he told me about his own challenge with his wife and how two of his children had died at infancy, the first at the age of two and the second at eleven months. He said he felt so sorry for his wife because they suffered so much to save their children but they surrendered all to God. They would eventually have a daughter and later a son while we were in Abuja. His wife graduated from the university and he also got a better job. I have seen them move above their family and social travails and are doing very well as they devote their time to the Lord.

I still needed a doctor to see Dike. I remembered Dr. Uju Bosah whom I had met in Chennai earlier in the year, so I called her. I needed Dike to see a Gastroenterologist (GIT) and she asked me to come with Dike to the National Hospital where she worked. We spent the whole day waiting to see a doctor but when it was time for me to pick my children from school, I had to leave. By the time we came back to the hospital, the doctors were rounding up seeing patients for the day. The attending General Practitioner asked us to come back early the next day so she could attend to us first. We came back the next day as advised but still spent the whole day waiting to see a doctor. We eventually saw the same doctor and she referred us to the Emergency Paediatric Unit (EPU.)

After another long wait at the EPU, we were again referred back to the Private Out-Patient Department (POPD). It was all so frustrating. Dike stooled constantly, the weather was extremely hot; the children were in school and I had no driver to assist me with driving as their school was quite a distance away, and home was remarkably far from the National Hospital. I also had no domestic help.

We finally got an appointment to see the GIT specialist the next week Wednesday, and I went to see Dr. Bosah with Dike who had started wheezing. She prescribed Coartem, a malaria medication, and paracetamol for him which I got from the hospital pharmacy, before we left to pick my girls from school. We got to their school late; I was completely exhausted but grateful that Doctor Bosah had attended to Dike.

We got home and I quickly dashed to the market to get some foodstuff to cook lunch. As I shopped, Amaka called to tell me that Dike had been crying uncontrollably ever since I left. I panicked and quickly got into the car to drive off, only to hear people around me shouting and pointing at my tyre. I stopped the car and as I opened my door, I heard a dog moan and limp away from behind the car. In my hurry to leave, I had run over a stray dog. The dog had crawled under my car to rest from the hot sun and as I reversed, my tire ran over its limb. I felt so terrible that my child had me rushing to him, but the poor stray dog that was hurt had no one to attend to it. As I drove off, I said a prayer for the dog's healing and I asked God to forgive me for hurting one of His creatures. I got home in good time, attended to Dike then went to the airport to pick Mike who was on his way from Port-Harcourt.

Given Dike's state of health, I needed to have a paediatrician who would attend to him in Abuja. I remembered my sister-in-law and friend Anyanna, whose son Deneval was born the same year I had Dalu in the USA. He had a complicated health challenge at birth and their phenomenal story was also a big miracle worth writing about. Anyanna lived in Abuja at that time with her family, and I felt she would have a good paediatrician for her son, so I called her and she told me she was presently at the clinic but the doctor was about to close for the day. She gave me the directions to the Abuja Clinic in the Maitama District and made the doctor wait for us as I hurriedly drove to meet them. Her son's paediatrician was a middle aged man called Dr. Awogu; I was glad we met him.

Dr. Awogu was quite compassionate and had Dike nebulized for his wheezing. He listened to Dike's history and he gave me meaningful advice on handling him. He also talked about the different options available for getting a liver transplant. He talked about some European and South American countries that were experimenting on harvesting the liver and promised to print some articles from the internet to help us in our search for Dike's cause.

We went home but had to go back to the hospital at night to nebulize Dike again; his breathing had become worse when we got home. I had no sleep but prayed all night. After I dropped the children off in school in the morning, I took him back to the clinic and the doctor requested for some more blood tests to further investigate his condition while he was given hydrocortisone injection and nebulized two more times. Fortunately, by nightfall he felt a lot better.

We were back in the hospital on Tuesday. The doctor had informed me that Dike's blood count had dropped from 12 to 10 and he had a viral infection, although he had stopped stooling and looked pale. He prescribed folic acid, multivitamins and oral rehydration solution to be included in his medication.

Anyanna had made an appointment for us to meet her pastor in another parish of the Redeemed Christian Church of God but on getting home we found a part of the house flooded with water from one of the showers which was left on. There had been no running water earlier and after the water was pumped, there was no one at home to turn off the taps. My security man and I ended up mopping the house; we did not go for the appointment with Anyanna.

That evening, my guest Chinelo who had come with her children and had been with us for over a week, rode with me to the pharmacy to pick up the prescribed medication for Dike, and to also check on a lady in church who had promised to get a domestic help for me. The service was already over by the time we got there, however the lady had not come to church. Pastor Ogan saw us and told us to come so he would pray for Dike. The other pastors joined in the prayers and anointed Dike with oil. It was a cold day and Dike had started wheezing again; the anointing was a very welcome solution for him. I stayed up all night as he wheezed; the wheezing eventually stopped at about 4.am.

Very early on the morning of Amaka's birthday, on 8th of October 2008, I dropped Mike off at Jabbi Express Road to get a taxi to the airport as he returned back to Port-Harcourt. I went home to take the children to school before going to the National Hospital for the appointment with the gastroenterologist.

We went to Amigo Supermarket to pick up a birthday cake for Amaka's celebration in school after we left the hospital and I ran into my brother, Emmanuel. We were pleasantly delighted to see each other, for we had last met when he visited us in Columbia, Maryland. He asked for an update on Dike's health which I gave him.

On Sunday the 19th of October 2008, I met my childhood friend S.B. Igwe in church and as we talked after the service; I asked after his sister Adaeze and was surprised and delighted when he told me that she was the assistant Pastor's wife. She had been one of those who received me well and had become very friendly over the past few weeks but she did not recognize me. I had met her husband Eke whom I had assumed was Yoruba because of his last name Aki, until our chance introduction in my house the day he and the other Senior Pastors came to dedicate our house. It turned out that Eke and my cousin Chudi Offor had both graduated from the University of Nigeria Nsukka and had been close friends. We hadn't seen each other in over 20 years and I was delighted to see him, especially as a pastor. It is a small world after all.

After S.B. and I met in church, Pastor Aki and his wife invited us over for lunch. S.B. was also there and we discussed Dike's condition. Having grown up in Enugu, I asked him if he knew a certain Dr. Perry Iloegbunam who was treating various ailments by exploring the stem cell method. Dr. Awogu had mentioned this to me and asked me to explore that option for Dike. S. B. took the name, found links to him and called later that night to give me his number.

I called Dr. Perry Iloegbunam and I was asked to forward all Dike's medical reports to their mailbox and pay the sum of N10,000.00 (Ten Thousand Naira) into their account as consultation fee. Mike paid the said sum and they later responded that Dike's condition was not such that they could handle.

God Has Spare Parts For His Creations

The church environment was our succour in those days as we settled down in Abuja. Dike was now 9 months old and moved around by crawling on his belly. He had learnt his first tangible word which was calling his sister Amaka. He never called her when she was in school, but once she came back from school, he would call her incessantly and clearly for the rest of the day.

During that period, I had also met a young couple, Richie and Iquo Emeni, and we became close friends. On hearing Dike's story, they insisted that we come to their church. Eventually after several weeks, on Wednesday the 22nd of October 2008, Dike and I went with them to Dayspring Bible Church to be prayed for by their pastor. I did this despite the fact that I had made up my mind not to subject my son to just anyone who claimed they had a solution for his ailment. I needed a lot of wisdom in handling Dike's health, and I believed that God would direct me to the right places of worship in the journey to strengthen my faith and for healing. I was not going to shop around for a miracle but I willingly decided to go to church with the Emeni family.

Due to the bureaucracy of the church, we were unable to see the senior pastor after the program/service and we left feeling somewhat discouraged. However, the service had been spirit filled with the theme "Breaking Ancestral Bonds". The senior pastor, Dr. Olowojoba, later called Richie and apologized for his inability to see us and asked that we come back during the week to see him after the service.

We went back to the church on Friday and saw him briefly at the back of the auditorium after the service. He laid hands on Dike and assured us that when the Lord heals, it is usually as easy as ABCD. He further said that if the manufacturers of Peugeot Automobile had the good sense to make spare parts for their product, then wouldn't the Almighty God have the ability to make spare parts for the body parts of all His creatures? He said he had experienced all manner of healings in his services including liver and kidney issues. He asked me if my friends told me he is a medical doctor and I replied that they had not. He then said that he is a medical doctor and understands what biliary atresia is but he wanted me to know that whatever the ailment, the Lord has the power to command all the organs to work perfectly. All he would ask me to do was to go home and praise God. I was elated and praised God as we left and I told him I was honoured to be the mother of my little boy because I was convinced that the Lord would use him in a mighty way.

I also told him that I had said to Dr. Subramania at the Apollo Hospital Chennai that I serve a God of miracles and was awaiting the manifestation of His grace in Dike's health. His words on the spare parts for God's creation gave me renewed hope whenever a new challenge emerged through our walk with Dike's health.

On Saturday the 25th of October 2008, the children and I went to the Yaradua Centre for my friend and in-law, Ifeatu Okeke's wedding. Many of our family friends and relations were shocked to see Dike looking jaundiced with a distended abdomen. My friend Anyanna, who is Ifeatu's younger sister, asked me to come to the high table to meet her sister-in-law, Mrs. Obioma Imoke the wife of the then Cross-Rivers State Governor. She introduced us and Mrs. Imoke immediately took Dike from me, turned her chair around and prayed for him; I was so touched by her kind gesture. She advised me to anoint him daily and as I did so, to also put a finger in the jar of oil and place some oil on his tongue. She told me that she would keep us in her prayers. As we left the wedding, I observed that Dike had become conscious of his hands and had started waving them. I praised God for an addition to his reflexes and strength despite the challenge.

On the 27th and 28th of October 2008, the children were on mid-term break so we all went to Port-Harcourt for the weekend; I worked tirelessly spring cleaning the house. My mother-in-law was at home and her health had deteriorated since we last saw her; this had become an additional cause of worry for Mike. After the weekend, we went back to Abuja. A few days later, I received a surprise telephone call from the chief paediatrician in the hospital where Dike was born. It was good to hear from her. She wanted an update on Dike's health which I gladly gave her. She wished us well as we ended our conversation.

On the 6th of November 2008, I finally got a maid and I was briefly relieved from the enormous domestic chores, and care for Dike and his siblings. That night however, I didn't get much sleep. It was now Dike's 10th month of life and the itch had become severe and was getting worse daily. I filed his nails every two days to prevent him from hurting his skin and eyes. Once more, I became frustrated having not received his feeding formula Dexolac, which I had ordered over a month earlier. He weighed 7.5kg and I was happy whenever I noticed a little increase in his weight.

I called Dr. V.S.S. to update him on his lab tests and the itching and he reintroduced a half tablet of Udiliv, three times daily and a quarter tablet of Vomikind twice daily into Dike's medication. Dike's bilirubin level had hit 315 i/u and the liver enzymes were now very high while the GGT remained low, which was the fundamental reason why the doctor remained convinced that Dike's liver disease was as a result of PFIC rather than biliary atresia.

On the 11th of November 2008, Dike finally agreed to eat his first solid meal which was okra soup and *eba*, our Nigerian meal. Sadly, the medication did not do much to relieve the itching which seemed to be worse around his genitals. His penis had become reddish yet jaundiced. His plight was worse at night and he would scream all through the midnight.

I took him to Abuja Clinics and Dr. Awogu told me he felt he had a urinary tract infection. We took some blood for tests and while I collected his urine for sampling, I observed that he was in severe pain while urinating which explained the screams. He was placed on a strong antibiotic Zinnat and on medication for malaria. I left the hospital feeling somewhat relieved that we now had some medication to ease Dike's pain.

It was time to pick the children from school. On my way out of the school, I met a friend in the car park and as we exchanged pleasantries, I lamented that the medication and formula I ordered for Dike were delayed and had not arrived. She scolded me for relying on medication for Dike's condition especially with all the pastors who had prayed for him. It was upsetting to be spoken to as if I was a faithless person despite everything I was going through. I walked away from her in anger and in tears for her lack of understanding; it is the person who wears the shoes that knows how it pinches.

I was hurt and could not put this encounter behind me. It troubled me and I thought about it all day. That evening, when I turned on the television to the Trinity Broadcasting Network channel, I listened to Jan Crouch talk about one's faith in healing and how the Lord had healed her of colon cancer a few years back. It was an insightful teaching and I began to feel peace in my spirit.

My brother Tonye came round later and I told him about the encounter I had with my friend earlier that day. Knowing Tonye's deep insight, I knew he would give me his candid opinion. He said I should not let my friend's opinion bother me, but to continue with Dike's medication for that was the right path to tread. He said that God gives people miracles through several ways and through medication one could also receive that grace of healing.

That weekend, the General Overseer, Pastor E. A. Adeboye was expected in Abuja for the special Holy Ghost Service. I had planned to go with Pastor Aki and his family but in my fatigued state I had to call it off, especially as Tonye had told me during his visit that he would seek an appointment with Pastor Adeboye for Dike's sake.

On Sunday the 16th of November 2008, I had a revelation on the problem I had with my Achilles heel. I recalled that during my pregnancy with Dalu, I had some very pronounced and painful varicose veins which gave me severe leg cramps. Most of the varicose veins disappeared after childbirth but they had re-emerged when I became pregnant again with Dike. After Dike's birth however, the varicose veins took a much longer time to clear.

Whilst in Chennai, Dr. Saravanah had diagnosed tendonitis as a result of the severe pain in my right Achilles' heel. He gave me an injection on the exact spot of the pain and by the time we got to the USA a month later, I had forgotten about the injection but noticed that my Achilles' heel was turning black. After a few days, the black skin started drying up and finally started peeling off like scales. My cousins and in-laws in the medical profession whom I showed the spot, did not know what it was but my sister-in-law, Vera prescribed triple action antibacterial ointment. Within two days of applying the ointment, the dead skin fell off and that part of my heel turned white.

I had a one-minute flashback that yielded a clear revelation which connected all the facets of the challenge I had with my Achilles heel, just like a jigsaw puzzle after many months of pain and distress. I had mental relief as I finally understood what it was that caused me so much discomfort.

Fast forward to a few years later, in the early dawn of 19th of September 2017, I received yet another revelation about the severe pain I had on my right leg - from my hip down to my toes - which began in early 2017, which could also be as a result of the severe varicose veins I had during my last two pregnancies.

Dike had taken ill the weekend of the Holy Ghost Service so we stayed at home; we watched the healing session of Dr. Chris Oyakhilome on the cable network. The next day in church, Pastor Faith, the music director carried Dike all through the praise and worship session and afterwards handed him over to Pastor Ogan who in turn carried him all through the rest of the service.

I was still concerned that his feeding formula Dexolac and the MCT oil had still not arrived. I had received a call from India informing me that the package had arrived Lagos on Monday but six days later, we had still not received it. Dike's appetite was very poor and his stool looked very lumpy, slimy and with black patches. We did not sleep very much, and I worried as he wheezed a lot and vomited the little food he was able to eat.

At the point of my exhaustion and despair, Dike woke up on Monday morning full of smiles. It was amazing and I gave glory to God for his happy demeanour. I was glad and knew it would be a good day despite his usual day long stooling. I took him back to see Dr. Awogu and after examining him, he said his condition seemed better than it was the previous week and his weight had gone up a bit from 7.6kg to 7.9kg. His haemoglobin had also risen to 9.7 from 8.7 the previous week. Having queried one of his tests, he requested that another sample be collected and gave a payment waiver which I was glad for.

The Visit To Pastor Adeboye

On Sunday the 7th of December 2008, Tonye called at about 5p.m. to inform me of the scheduled 10am appointment the next day with the General Overseer of the Redeemed Christian Church of God, Pastor E. A. Adeboye in Lagos. With Tonye's arrangement, we took an early flight to Lagos the next morning and arrived at the RCCG Church Headquarters at 9.45am. We were ushered in to see Daddy G.O. as he is fondly called. It was 10.20am. His office was very spacious and had various ecclesiastical objects that symbolized his life's purpose.

When Daddy G.O. met with us, he expressed shock on seeing us with this very handsome baby who had a liver condition and his expression was simply humbling, which was very characteristic of him.

"This small boy? So young," said Daddy G.O.

He asked me to put Dike down on his table which I did and he laid his hands on Dike's abdomen and prayed, asking God to fix what needed to be fixed and replace what needed to be replaced. He prophesied that Dike would live to serve the Lord and will have a testimony in the New Year by the grace of God and we would have cause to testify in the Redeemed Camp. We returned back to Abuja immediately after seeing Daddy G.O.

On Sunday the 14th of December 2008, we were back in Abuja and had a guest speaker in church who held an anointing service. I testified to the church about Ugonna's distinction in her school results despite being the youngest in her class and falling sick during the examination period. I also testified that Dike would be one year in three weeks' time despite his small frame, praying the Lord would sustain us in strength and in good looks despite the daily stress we passed through.

After the service, a family friend of the Ikeazor's who was visiting from Florida, spoke to me and encouraged me with her own daughter's testimony. Her daughter was born with the sickle cell disease and had to undergo a bone-marrow transplant and afterwards, her genotype changed to AA. She said God used her daughter to perform a medical first, therefore I should be encouraged to go ahead and seek a liver transplant for my son.

"All shall be well," she said to me with a smile.

I appreciated her words of advice and encouragement, and also her courage in her own daughter's life struggle.

Christmas Holidays

The children's school went on vacation for the Christmas holidays on the 16th of December 2008 after their Christmas party and carol. Unfortunately, I missed the event as I had to sort out some domestic issues. Dalu and Amaka were very disappointed, and I was sad for missing out on such a great event.

We left Abuja for Port Harcourt to spend the first eight days of the holiday, then went to our home town in Ekwulobia on the 26th of December 2008 for the rest of the holidays.

Our stay in the village was very traumatic and became a major family crisis due to some very ignorant family members who, rather than try to understand our challenge with Dike, chose to spread malicious rumours about the issues that besieged us.

My husband and I were very hurt by the actions of those who chose not to understand medical advancement and the optimism we had in the face of our son's challenge. I was once more convinced that through this additional challenge, Dike would be made a hero, for he already had God's anointing. I reassured myself with the Bible verse that states:

> 'Touch not my anointed."
> 1 Samuel 26:8

I was also convinced that the trauma we faced would make Dike's story complete and shame the devil. I knew the journey would not be a smooth one. I made up my mind not to bear a grudge against anyone, for I would not allow anyone make me sin by making me so angry so as to end up in hell.

I left our village home with the children and three of my decorating team on the 29th of December 2008 for my maternal grandmother's home in Oba, which is within the state, to celebrate her 95th birthday. We also had my maternal grand uncle's funeral to attend and my team were on hand to decorate for both events.

We had a full house and despite the fun of the yuletide, Dike's condition allowed me no sleep. He itched and cried endlessly and my family members who witnessed this were very sympathetic to our plight and gave words of encouragement.

Two remarkable people were at home that season; one was my second cousin Ugochukwu, who flew in from the U.K. I was very glad to see that he had turned into a fine gentleman, and was about to graduate from college. The other person was my cousin Constance, who is also Ugochukwu's first cousin. It was a beautiful reunion for all of us, especially for the two who had never been home during a festive period as they both lived abroad and never had the opportunity to meet and mingle with their extended families.

Just before midnight on the 31st of December 2008, we held a marvellous prayer session at my Aunt May's country home which was led by Tonye. The Bible text was taken from Joshua 1:1-9 with the memory verse:

> "Though thy beginning was small, yet thy latter end shall greatly increase."
> Job 8: 7

The prediction was that the year would be a very difficult one with tougher challenges but for those who trust in the Lord, they would overcome.

It was the first of January 2009. I went with my cousins Constance and Ugochukwu to see some of our extended families. We saw my great uncle Beacon Onwuamaegbu whom I occasionally spent weekends with at his home in Aba during my years as an undergraduate. I had not seen him in years and he had aged but was in good care. I was delighted that despite his condition he recognised me, and even asked after my elder brother. He eventually passed away in 2016 when he was almost a hundred years old.

It was Dike's first holiday in the village and he was coping well despite the itchiness, especially at night. There were many family members to visit during our stay and we knew we might not be able to see everyone.

On the 3rd of January 2009, we visited Mike's aunt Lady Maudeline in the neighbouring town of Nanka. She advised me not to give in to the schemes of the devil who was on a mission to tear our family apart. She therefore urged me to forgive all the family members who had caused us pain in order to let peace reign, for it was only through genuine forgiveness that the devil's schemes could be thwarted.

Our holiday over, Mike drove us back to Abuja on the 5th of January 2009. It was a long fifteen hour journey and we arrived home exhausted. On a good day, the journey would have taken about eight hours, but the roads were busy as many people were returning to their various locations within and outside Nigeria after the Christmas holidays.

We were lucky our house was not layered in dust as is usual at that time of the year due to the dry, dusty harmattan weather, so we were able to unpack and settle in without having to clean the house first.

It was the 7th of January 2009, Dike's first birthday. We awoke that morning praising God and thanking Him for Dike's life. It was very emotional for me. I was pleasantly surprised when my uncle, Dr. Ibe called to inform me that he was sending a young girl to me as a domestic help and I had to go pick her up from the bus station. I was delighted and very grateful to him for going the extra mile to get me help, even though I had not told him directly that I needed one, my aunt Stella had mentioned it to him.

I had invited a few of our friends to come celebrate Dike's birthday with us and I had to go to the market to buy foodstuff to cook. I thought I could co-ordinate that with the young girl's pickup but unfortunately that didn't work out and I had to leave the bus station to go prepare for our celebration. She finally found her way to the house after she arrived and called me for directions.

Our party of about five families went well. Notably present were the Emeni's, the Okaros, the Imokes, the Akis and my Aunt May's family. Dike as usual slept into the early hours of the morning after a restless, itchy and weepy night. I often anointed him and continuously asked God for His grace to endure the plight, as we both remained totally stressed out.

The Open Heavens devotional message for that day 7th of January 2009 was titled "A New Thing" with text taken from Isiah 43:19 which read:

"Behold I will do a new thing: now it shall spring forth: shall ye not know it? I will even make a way in the wilderness, and rivers in the desert."
Isaiah 43:19.

Planning Our Return To India

We had to go back to India for Dike's check-up and we planned our trip for the 29th of January 2009. Dr V.S.S. had asked Dr. Neelam Mohan, the liver consultant in New Delhi, to send us an invitation letter. As I prepared to go to the Indian High Commission, I received e-mail from Dr. Neelam's mail informing us that it was India's Republic Day so the invitation letter would be sent the next day. Due to some technical hitches, our visas were issued a day later so I re-booked our tickets for the 30th of January 2009.

On Wednesday the 28th of January 2009, as I prepared Dike's cocktail of medication, I suddenly realised that his Ondansetron/Vormikind was finished. I was alarmed once more and wondered how I would cope if he began to itch all over again. My only solution was to pray. I had peace after praying and the assurance that all would be well. I realised afterwards that the Lord had given us another grace after Dr. Olowojoba had prayed and the night sweat had actually stopped. Prior to that meeting, I would usually change Dike's pyjamas about three times each night. It was as if his body was a sponge that continued to ooze out water every three hours while he slept. Dike did not itch the entire time until we returned to India.

On Thursday before our trip, Dike, Dalu, Amaka and I went to see Ugonna at the Turkish International College. She was all weepy and I pacified her, reminding her on the need to remain prayerful and faithful for I believed that all will be well.

I had made an arrangement with a sister in church, Sister Onyekachi Uduku who had visited me in Port-Harcourt and having heard of Dike's challenge, offered to move in to live with the children whilst I was away in India. She would also visit Ugonna two days later for her school's Cultural Day and also go on her visiting days later in the term.

Later in the afternoon, I went to the Indian High Commission to pick up our visas and was told they were not ready but would be the next day. I was apprehensive and I could not afford to move our tickets one more day as I earnestly needed to get Dike out because we had exhausted his anti-itch medication. Changing our tickets again would mean rescheduling our local flight to Lagos and also the outbound international flights which would be surcharged. I silently prayed for favour as I waited for the visas to be issued. After waiting for about an hour, I called my brother Tonye to brief him and ask him to pray with me. Shortly afterwards, as some of us intending travellers refused to leave the High Commission without our visas, the Charge d' Affairs addressed us saying those with proof of travel within 24 hours should stay back to be issued with visas. I had no proof for I had left our tickets at home, but the man just took a look at me and asked the lady in charge to stop all she was doing and attend to me first. That was favour from God once more.

We travelled on Friday but missed our scheduled 10.15am flight due to heavy traffic on the way to the airport so we rebooked our flight. Eventually it turned out that our earlier flight was actually delayed, as were all the other flights, as a result of the extraordinary traffic on that day.

As we settled to board, I met a family friend Miebi Aguma who was on her way to Dubai, and we went together from the local to the International airport. She was very shocked and sympathetic to hear of the issues concerning Dike. We had a smooth flight to Dubai and I met my distant cousin Ebele Onwuamegbu on the flight. It was good to see her after over two and a half decades. We chatted quite a bit during the flight as we had a lot of catching up to do. We had a brief stopover in Dubai and we were once again airborne to Chennai.

The Open Heavens devotional for the 30th of January 2009 was apt. It was titled "Dr. Jesus" and the text was from Genesis 18: 9 – 14. The message stated that the Lord deliberately delayed Sarah and Abraham from conceiving a child till their old age. He also delayed healing Lazarus so that He could maximize the glory. God's time is always the best; irrespective of what we are going through, He is always on time. He is the restorer of life therefore he is never too early or too late.

CHAPTER 4

Return To Chennai

I was thrilled to see Ken, Nathalie and Joshua at the airport to receive Dike and I. We went straight to Sea Shell Residency where we had stayed on our previous trip to Chennai. I would have preferred somewhere else but Ken advised that we stayed there for security reasons. After they left us, Dike and I stayed up cleaning out the room and sorting our belongings till 1.30am when we finally fell asleep, exhausted.

We woke up at 8.30am, having fed Dike twice during our slumber. Ken took us to see Dr. V.S.S. and he was quite happy to see us. He told us that his son who had been in Australia was back and would attending to us in his private clinic. We left to have lunch in the lovely Chinese restaurant we had been to with Mike on our previous visit. Afterwards, we went to Apollo Hospital to see the International Patient's office staff we had been acquainted with on our earlier visit.

Jithu, Nivi, Sneha and Sonnalika and most of the others were there but Nithya whom I also really wanted to see had left. Some of them were surprised that I still remembered their names and they were all excited to see that Dike was still in good health. I was told that Dr. Subramaniam had left the hospital and relocated to the United States. Jithu suggested we see Dr. Khakar but his phone lines were not reachable. We later went back to Sea Shell Residency and took a 30-minute nap before getting ready to go back to Dr. V.S.S's clinic to meet with his son, Dr. Srinivas.

We met Dr. Srinivas whom his father had passionately talked about on our earlier visit. Dr. V.S.S. had told us that his son was also a medical doctor practicing in Australia and had said he would send him details of Dike's history. On meeting Doctor Srinivas, it seemed to us that we already knew him and I told him so. He was impressed to see that Dike had gained some weight at 8.7kg. He said that any weight above 8kg for Dike's age was okay for a liver transplant. He reminded me that there was only one option for us in India which was the option of a living donor, as there was no choice of a cadaveric donor. This being the result of the beliefs and practices of majority of Indians who would rather go to the great beyond with their body parts intact.

Dr. Srinivas promised to discuss with his father and Dr. Neelam Mohan, and then call me later in the night. He prescribed Simyl MCT formula and asked that I discontinue Dexolac and MCT oil. He assured me that the formula was better than Dexolac but might be difficult to find in Chennai since the company that produced it had left the city. He would discuss with his father to see how they would aid us to procure a reasonable quantity of the formula.

After the meeting, Ken left while Dike and I went back to our hotel. I slept at 2am and woke at 11.30am although I woke to feed Dike twice during the night. It was indeed the longest and best sleep I had in a long while.

At that point in time, I reflected on the devotional of 30th of January 2009 titled "Dr. Jesus" which reminded us that there is a greater doctor called Jesus. In Genesis 18:14, The Lord said to Sarah "is anything too hard for the Lord?" God is one who is never too late.

"Does it seem that God is appearing late in your situation? Does He seem not to hear your cries? Are you thinking of throwing in the towel? Don't! He will intervene in your situation at the right time for His time is best; for He is always on time. He is never too early nor too late," said Pastor Adeboye in the message for the day.

The devotional told the story of a wounded war veteran who had died and then came back to life. He later became very sick and was abandoned in a church where the pastor and members ran away because of the stench that came out of him. Dr. Jesus and some nurses came and operated on him and while he watched the operation of his decaying intestines being removed and replaced, not a drop of blood nor scar was visible. The Lord reminded us with the question, "Is there anything too difficult for me?"

On Tuesday the 3rd of February 2009, I spoke to my aunt, Dame Adeline, and I was exceedingly glad when she told me she would come to India and donate her liver to save Dike. This gesture like a few others, once more brought me to tears but also to a point of prayer and thanksgiving for the grace the Lord had planted in the hearts of His people to share in our emotional burden. I was excited knowing that my loved ones stood with me, but then I also knew the reality of the impossibility of the offer from my aunt. She was a bit advanced in age to be a donor; she was in her early sixties and fifty-three was the maximum age for a donor. I later spoke to my aunt Dr. Nwosu who is Dame Adeline's immediate younger sister, and she suggested putting up a mail on Ikolink which is my maternal family yahoo group, to ask our family members for a willing donor.

I saw Dr. Srinivas again and was amazingly surprised when he told me that Dr. Neelam Mohan is female and not male as I had earlier thought. From the conversation they had, she had advised that I should not come over to Delhi if I did not have a donor for Dike. There were specifications listed about the potential donor and they were facts she wanted me to have foreknowledge of.

Above all, a donor had to be a blood relative and the DNA of the donor had to be checked and matched with the patient's for confirmation. Once more, I was left in a state of confusion yet totally trusting God to make a way in our hopeless situation. Later, Ken took us to the shop called Just Born and I got the different packaged meals for Dike including his favourite Gerber's sweet potato and corn meal.

Later that day, I spoke to my brother Emmanuel who was in Philadelphia with his mother and his children. He asked me what blood group was required for eligibility to donate liver to Dike. I told him that Dike is B+ and he said he is A+ like me; therefore he would not be eligible to donate. He gave me the good news that his daughter Nkeiru was getting married on the 14th of February. I also spoke to his mother and she told me they were continually praying for us.

On Thursday the 5th of February 2009, we did a liver function test and the GGT had gone up to 50 IU/L. The total bilirubin was at 20.8 mg/dL, the bilirubin direct was 12.2 mg/dL while the bilirubin indirect was 8.6 mg/dL. SGOT was 500 IU/L and the SGPT was 190 IU/L. The alkaline phosphate was 1370 IU/L. These figures were alarming, and I became troubled and felt helpless once more. I knew we were running out of time but once again I reflected on the messages of the week and peace engulfed me. I recalled the numerous revelations and confirmations which would lead to the restoration after the trials.

Dr. Srinivas asked me to discontinue Renewliv, for he did not think there was any more benefit from it for Dike. Dike still itched and it bothered me why these medications were being discontinued. Again, the Simyl MCT had an unpleasant smell and taste and I was tempted to give Dike the Dexolac every now and then.

There were sleepless nights but I knew the doctors understood what was best for Dike's condition. We later consulted with Dr. V.S.S.'s wife who is also a paediatrician. Dr. Neelam had advised that we took all the childhood vaccines. I paid 2500 Rupees and had Dike take all the shots for hepatitis A and chicken pox. We left and went to Jithu's office in Apollo Hospital to check my mails and see if Dr. Neelam had replied the frequently asked questions Mike had sent to her.

While there, I received a call from my late mother's close friend, Aunty Ifeoma Egbuonu a professor in paediatrics. She was disappointed that I had not called to tell her about our challenge with Dike's health. We spoke at length and she later asked for Mike's number so she could have a discussion with him. After we spoke, I called Mummy Meg for she had been anxious to hear from us and wondered what was causing the delay in finding a solution. She assured me that she was upholding us in her prayers, which I knew was her daily chore for us.

Jithu insisted I see Dr. Aanand Khakar, so we went to find him; we met him on the staircase. He suggested we do an assessment so Dike could be placed on a waiting list, for he said they occasionally had cadavers in the Chennai branch of the Apollo Hospital. He stressed that it was not possible to get cadavers in Delhi. I did not bother with Apollo Hospital as I had made up my mind to head to

Delhi to meet with Dr. Neelam Mohan whether I had a donor or not.

The Open Heavens of Saturday 7th of February 2009 was titled "Bodily Evidence of Love" with text taken from Ephesians 5: 25–33. The text is a command to husbands to love their wives. The action point stated: "Take a good look at your wife and identify all the physical and psychological scars you have brought on her. Lovingly compensate her for each".

The message moved me to tears; I was going through so much pain and I thought of my husband so far away in Nigeria. In the state I was in, I knew it was only Christ that would give me the desired comfort I needed.

I went back to Jithu's office and opened my mailbox and found a letter from Mike stating his confusion about Dike's situation. He wanted my candid opinion and I wrote him a detailed reply. For the sake of posterity, I made it clear that I am not the one to take a decision for him. Those were very critical moments in our relationship as we had our different views and opinions. I just wanted to do what I understood was the will of God especially with the numerous revelations I had. He was going through his own personal challenges as the head of the home and it was an unnerving time for both of us and the stress was becoming obvious. I had tried my best to explain how I felt and to let him understand my fears, as we were both in pain and hurting badly. We needed the grace of God and a lot of wisdom to help us overcome our situation and move forward. I knew our apprehension could cause a strain in our relationship which we could not afford to have at the time.

I clearly understood that God usually gives one person a vision for a specific purpose. I had no doubt that one could go through so many obstacles to convince people to key into the vision but with a lot of perseverance and determination, the vision would eventually become clearer and could become actualized. I refused to be confused but remained focused with an unflinching belief that the end would be great despite the situation at hand.

Who Will Cry When You Die

Tonye called me on Sunday the 8th of February 2009 at 3.45am and we spoke for about 30 minutes about Dike's situation. We were both convinced that God had a hand in what was happening; the reason was yet to unfold. I told him my spiritual stand on the situation and that I am a mere custodian to Dike. I was willing to do my best as directed by the Almighty so that His will concerning Dike will be done. Tonye agreed with me and I told him about the book I was reading which I had bought at the Apollo Hospital Bookshop.

I had bought a number of books by Robin Sharma and they had been the most interesting and inspiring books I had read in a long time. The principles in Sharma's writings were positively life influencing. *Who Will Cry When You Die?* and *The Monk Who Sold His Ferrari* were the first two of his books I was reading at that time. Tonye's conclusion was that if Dike has a sudden healing it might not result in a spiritual uplifting which we needed very much, rather God knew the pattern to follow to bring about the much desired humility, atonement and peace we needed. I went back to sleep at 6am after our talk, while Dike had slept earlier on at about 3.15am.

Dike and I finally woke at 9.30am and we got ready for the Sunday service. Ken, Nathalie and their son Joshua came in a taxi at 11.00am and we went with them to The Assemblies of God Church where they worshipped. The sermon was given by a guest preacher whose message was that God knows why He allows certain things to happen the way they do in our lives.

The minister said that his father was a driver who had managed to send him to good schools, although he could only afford to wear second hand clothes which gave him a complex in those days, considering that his classmates all came from affluent families. He later made it to the United States and went into business; he held up the values his father had instilled in him and those he inculcated from school, and had become very successful.

He became a born again Christian at age sixteen and started pastoring a church soon after. He said he had travelled around the world preaching the gospel and now God had brought him back to his roots in India. He further stated that the Lord had exposed him to so much money, to the rich and to the western world at an early age for the sole purpose of equipping him to preach all over the world, to the very rich especially and also not to have a complex about his humble beginnings.

The beauty in his excellent message was that these lessons were also the confirmation of what Tonye and I had discussed into the early morning that Sunday. The preacher had said there was always a reason why God delays, not because He cannot deliver on our expectations but because He knows our weaknesses. He would rather answer us at the right time, for He would not want to break us but to rather purify us through the challenge.

In Dike's case, I was convinced it was so we would be pushed to the wall before we make new affirmations concerning our lives. As I pondered on the situation at hand, I recalled a quote thus:

> "If a man has not discovered something that he will die for, he isn't fit to live."
> Martin Luther King Jr.

I believe that one should not love life so much such as to desperately hold onto it. We must let go and let God.

After the Sunday service, we went to the beach at the shore of the Indian Ocean and Nathan and Dike played in the sand. We went through St. Thomas, which was the modernized early church built by Thomas the disciple of Jesus.

We returned to the hotel later in the afternoon and I gave Dike a bath. Shortly afterwards, Jithu and his wife Achu took us to dine at a Chinese restaurant in Nungambakkam not too far from the Apollo Hospital. After dinner, as we came out of the elevator in the restaurant, two Indian families waiting to get into the elevator took a look at us and were enchanted by Dike. They begged to carry him and I gave him to them; they played with him for a while.

"If only they knew the challenge awaiting the cute child they had just carried," I said to myself as we left.

Thinking of the two Indian families, their politeness and humility in expressing their affection towards a child they did not know, a child from a different race and one who was going through a medical challenge they did not even know about, overwhelmed me. Right there, the Lord revealed to me that the child these kind strangers were carrying was a star in the making. My Dike. I had that inner feeling and conviction that all would be well. I felt so honoured to be the mother of Diken'agha, the mighty warrior in battle.

Vivi And Medya

On Wednesday the 11th of February 2009, I met a Nigerian lady, Ifeoma Vivian Okoli at the International Patients' office of the Apollo Hospital. She took me to her room in the Apollo Annex building and I was quite surprised that a nice place like that was available to the patients. It was even cheaper and more convenient than Sea Shell Residency and the menu from the hospital restaurant, which I also did not know about, was quite appetizing. I was surprised the International office had not informed me of this accommodation especially as I had complained to them several times about the food while on admission with Mike on our first visit a few months earlier. Vivian promised to look out for a room once an occupying patient was discharged.

When we went back to the International Services office, I met Medya Musungu, a Kenyan whose sixteen year old daughter had a prolonged liver disease and had just undergone a liver transplant; she was now in intensive care. She took me to see her charming daughter in the ICU and we dressed up in scrubs to see her. Her daughter was so soft spoken and charming. We spoke briefly; I encouraged her and prayed with them. She told me she loved Dr. Khakar for saving her life and she would love to be a liver transplant surgeon someday to save lives like he had saved hers.

We left and Medya and I talked about the liver transplant procedure. She showed me her sutures which was alarming; nevertheless I felt the surgery was worth doing to save a loved one. She asked for Mike's e-mail address to communicate with him on her experience and possibly let him know one person who had gone through the process of liver donation. Later that night, she called me to say that Mike did reply her e-mail and had confessed he was actually worried.

The next day, I had an appointment with the specialists and met with Dr. Mrs. Malathy Satyasekavan. She was the paediatric hepatologist in Apollo Hospital and I was very impressed with her diagnosis. She looked at Dike and said his ailment was clearly a case of PFIC2 for if it was biliary atresia, degradation would have set in. She was very convinced that Dike had a liver disease rather than a blocked bile duct. I was glad to hear this; she was the second doctor, apart from Dr. V.S.S., to conclude this fact based on Dike's presentation and his medical reports. She said she would not cause Dike any more discomfort by allowing him go through further investigations but would study all the reports we already had from The Child Trust Hospital.

Dike had developed a fever a day earlier so she prescribed malaria drugs and she asked us to do a few more tests before administering the cocktail of medication she was going to prescribe. They were Questran, Kenadion and Evion drops, which were the same medication Dr. Srinivas had discontinued. I was glad she put Dike back on these medications especially as he was still itching. She said Dike had a little time which was also a major difference between the biliary atresia children and the PFIC 2 ones. I left her office a lot happier than when I went in, believing that all would be well.

I went back to the International Patient's office to check my e-mails. Mike had sent a mail informing me he would come to India at the end of the month and was already on his way to Abuja for his Indian visa.

Friday the 13th of February 2009 was our 14th day in India and also the deadline for our immigration clearance. Jithu asked the driver Mr. Saravanah to take me to the Immigration Office for the clearance. I met again with Mrs. Vivian Okoli at the hospital. It turned out her family and mine had greater family ties; her father was an old friend of my uncle Chib. In any case, she had secured a room for me at the Apollo annex and I quickly moved my things before going to the Immigration office.

Some hours later, Cousin Dike called me from the United States and we talked for a while. Talking with him always soothed me; for indeed he remains a cousin who sticks closer than a brother.

Later that evening, Dike became very restless and was in pain. He was itching all over and his bum had been red all week; this was a frequent occurrence and I was using Canesten cream to treat it as usual. This time however, I realised he was scratching his groin very badly and I also observed that he only had a few droplets of urine in his diaper. He had also started stooling more frequently. It was unnerving. I called Mrs. Vivian into our room to pray with me and afterwards I called Dr. Joi, a young doctor who had examined Dike earlier in the day. I had the wisdom to always ask the attending doctors for their numbers for I never knew when the next emergency would be.

I was glad Dr. Joi was still in the hospital, so I rushed Dike to the paediatric unit. She suspected he had a urinary tract infection and immediately administered some medication to make him sleep. She advised I give him a lot of water to drink then have a urine test done early in the morning. I exposed his bum so he would be free and heal faster. In the morning, Dr. Satyasekavan saw us in the ward and later discharged us as Dike had stabilized over the night.

I went in search of a travel agency and found one within the neighbourhood. I bought a one way ticket on Jet Air to New Delhi, for Chennai no longer had any opportunities for us regarding what we sought; I knew it was time to go. I called Dr. Srinivas to inform him that we were headed out to Delhi as he had been in touch with

Dr. Neelam Mohan. She had made all our logistics arrangements including a pickup from the airport even though she still wondered what we were coming to do in Delhi without a donor.

My spirit was strong and quickened to go and I knew there was hope. In blind faith, I went in obedience as I remembered the scripture in Genesis 22 where Abraham had taken his son Isaac to the mountain to sacrifice, but the Lord gave him a ram for the sacrifice instead. I also held on to the Book of Life and its promises in Joshua 1:8-9.

We arrived Delhi and were taken to the Royal Palace Hotel in Rajinder Nager. We were received and taken up to our room. The hotel had an ancient elevator and a dim hallway which made me very nervous and uncomfortable. It had been a long and exhausting day - from the Chennai hospital activities, packing for our trip, carrying a baby with frequent feeds, itchiness, change of clothes and diapers, the fifty-minute flight delay, the two and a half hour flight plus the commuting to and fro the airports. I was not pleased to be in such an uncomfortable hotel.

I tried to settle into our room for the night, yet despite being as tired as I was, I could not rest as the room had an unpleasant smell and felt unclean. I could not go to another hotel because it was already past 8pm and rather late in an unfamiliar terrain. I was stuck and miserable in that hotel especially after our hospitable experience in the Apollo Hospital. I eventually asked to have my room changed when I could bear the discomfort no longer. I was given a room on the ground floor and I felt a lot better and I relaxed a bit. I said my prayers, managed to document my days' journey, and afterwards I fell asleep with no choice but to cover up with the blanket the hotel provided to shield my son and I from the winter cold.

We got up early on Monday the 16th of February 2009 and went for our 11.30am appointment with Dr. Neelam. It was a five-minute walk from the hotel to the Sir Ganga Ram Hospital reception and I carried Ḍike as usual in the carrier bag across my chest. We arrived Dr. Neelam's office and her office assistant, Sweeti Kundra received us. We also met Dr. Neelam's secretary Kanta Bhatai; these two ladies would later become my closest allies all through our stay in India. Both got married a few years later, Kanta still works with Dr. Neelam and I have remained in touch with them.

Meeting The Diva

Sweeti ushered me into a small conference room to await the arrival of "Maam", as she called Dr. Neelam Mohan. After about fifteen minutes, the door suddenly was opened by a swift walking, small framed, beautiful lady. She walked in with two men carrying sophisticated cameras and video equipment. I got up, smiled and politely greeted her and the two camera men.

"You must be Chi," she said, as she settled into a chair.

I was awed by her ambience. She excused herself and faced the camera men as she talked to them while they recorded and took pictures of her in various poses. I was magnetized by her speech, and her total demeanour for in front of me was a highly intelligent, fulfilled and exciting lady. As I listened to her talk, I saw her as a Diva and I wondered what medical feat had been achieved that made the cameramen come after her.

At some point, she paused and possibly knowing what I was thinking, turned to me and explained; the cameramen were journalists from CNN and the BBC who had come to interview her after the medical feat she and her team had achieved with the first domino liver transplant case. She said the surgery involved three persons - two children with different liver disorders and an aunt of one of the children. She asked if I had seen the newspaper headlines in the past few days. Unfortunately, I had not read the papers nor listened to the news due to the pressure I was under at that time.

She went on to explain the medical conditions of the two children, Shourya Verma and Thakur Siya why their cases were unique and the excitement in the medical world and especially the reason for the media coverage. It was India's first and the world's youngest domino liver transplant. (https://www.indiabookofrecords.in) Being in the company of Dr. Neelam was great and as she passionately talked about the feat; I had no doubt that I was at the right place at the right time. I was convinced that the Lord had ordered my steps to meet with this great lady on that day and at that exact moment, a lady whom I would later call my friend. I mumbled a prayer to God that He should use Dr. Neelam and her team to also have a medical breakthrough with Dike, so we would also have a cause to celebrate as I had just witnessed in that room.

The Lord heard that humble prayer and I knew without doubt that my writings and struggles would not be in vain.

After the two men had left, Dr. Neelam asked that I move into the hospital with Dike to enable her start the investigations on him. At 5.pm, I moved our luggage into room 1027 of the paediatric ward D.

Day 2. I took Dike for a scan then afterwards, Dr. Neelam did an endoscopy. She explained to me that there are four stages in the liver degeneration; Dike was between the second and the third stage which meant the liver disease was at an advanced stage.

The PKKT, which is a thrombose test, was done and she said the result was not so good although one of the films seemed okay. She would give Dike a vitamin K injection although he had taken one in Chennai from Dr. Mrs. V.S.S.

Dr. Neelam said she would wait for some other results in order to decide if she would go ahead with a biopsy of Dike's liver. She later decided to go ahead with the biopsy. Afterwards, she sent the slide abroad for analysis to determine the exact ailment Dike suffered. She knew that a transplant was unavoidable.

Later in the day, Dr. Neelam came to our room with some of the liver transplant team. As we discussed, I told her that Dike had taken the vaccines she had prescribed through Dr. Srinivas except the MMR (Measles Mumps and Rubella.) Dr. Neelam explained that Dike ought to have taken all the vaccines on time because if they needed to go ahead with the transplant then we would need to wait for three weeks thus a delay of three week would mean a prolonged stay in India and some additional upkeep costs to us.

She explained to me the need to always trust and obeyed her opinion and judgement to enable her do her job well and that if I ever found myself in doubt, I should call her for a clarification. She advised that Dike's donor be available the following week for a few days of assessment.

The team left the room and as Dr. Neelam was leaving last, I walked her out to the stairs and as we said our goodbyes I whispered to her,

"If only I could donate my liver to save my son."

Dr. Neelam abruptly turned to face me.

"Chi, what did you say?"

I looked at her firmly and repeated the statement I had just mumbled.

"Are you serious?" She asked, looking at me as if I had said something unbelievable.

"Yes Maam," I said with tears in my eyes.

She asked again if I was serious and willing to donate my liver to save my son. I gave her the affirmation that I would if I could.

"I have never seen such faith," she said as she embraced me. "Chi, I will do all I can to save your son. Today I have seen that you have such great faith and that you have a strong spirit. Your spirit has mingled with mine, and I will do all I have to do in order to help save your son."

She turned to embrace me. I was overcome by my emotions and I wept.

"Chi, just tap into my energy," she said as she embraced me again. "I hope you pray," she said as she released me from her embrace.

On hearing this statement, I immediately felt a great relief. Peace engulfed me as we turned in opposite directions.

She took a step down, paused and looked up at me.

"Don't discuss this with anyone, no one whatsoever, not even with my team and no one close to you. Let this be the pact between us two and heaven as we await a solution for saving Dike. We will be silent about this till God gives us the wisdom to know what to do," she said to me quietly.

I went back into the room totally stunned by another encounter with the other side of the incredible Dr. Neelam whom I call the Diva.

The statement I made became one that would oil the wheel of change in the situation we were in. It also became the bedrock of friendship and trust between Dr. Neelam and I. I understood her authority in the medical profession, her faithfulness, her call as a paediatrician, her loyalty to her patients and her colleagues, her total devotion to her work, and eventually her love for her family and mankind. I have never met a more incredible woman in my life, as I watched her over the months and years. Although we are of different religious beliefs, she Hindu and I Christian, our mutual respect for each other created a great aura and positive energy to work as a team to achieve a common goal.

The nurses came to take Dike for some more blood tests. He had been pricked from morning till night and as we ate our dinner they came again for more blood.

Dr. Neelam came back that night to tell me that Dike had a fever which was obvious from the results of his blood tests, therefore she would start him on some antibiotics and would include the Vitamin D injection. She still asked for some more blood to be drawn. He was given the tuberculosis vaccine before the Vitamin D injection. Dike weighed 9.3 kg at one year and six weeks of age. We were happy that he had added some weight since our return to India as he was better managed. Dr. Neelam suggested taking my own samples for Hepatitis B tests.

A new day, and the investigations continued. Dr. Neelam explained to me that Dike's veins were very narrow and would likely make the surgery very difficult and more challenging. A nuclear scan and a C.T scan were required to ascertain the exact size of his features and bone density. The result of these confirmed the doctor's thought of about 2" instead of the expected 6" for his age. The thyroid specialist also said that the results were irregular and he sent the samples back to be re-tested. I showed her the reports from Apollo Hospital which showed no abnormality.

Later in the day the tall handsome and remarkable Surgeon Dr. A.S. Soin who was the head of the liver transplantation unit of the Sir Ganga Ram Hospital came with some of his team including Dr. Neelam Mohan to welcome us and I was very excited to meet him. I congratulated him on their great team work; and especially on the domino liver transplant success they had just celebrated with the media conference.

Dike's liver biopsy report was out and it revealed that his liver had become so cirrhotic that a transplant was urgently required. Dr. Neelam told me she was glad I made the choice to come to their hospital because at any other hospital, especially the specialists in cadaveric transplants, they would probably not know what to do with him. He was given Influenza vaccine as well as some other injections.

Zaheera

A few days after our admission, Dr. Neelam came to my room to tell me that a lady named Zaheera from my country had come to the hospital with her son for a liver transplant. I later met her along the corridor and decided to visit her later in the day. She told me she is South African and I was amused because Dr. Neelam always referred to anyone from Africa as my sister or brother. Zaheera looked like a white Indian and her son Azhar was also very light skinned about Dike's age. In fact she looked more like a sister to Dr. Neelam's than a sister to me. She had come in company of her husband Ashraf, their two daughters and her own mother who was an option for the donor. She and her son were admitted in a room adjacent to ours.

Nursing a child on admission in hospital was a lot of work. There was so much to learn about dispensing medication to the child and the total care required. With Dike, the frequent stooling and frequent feeding, left me with very little time to chat or even read.

On our seventh day on admission, I finally went over to see Zaheera and her family with Dike. We both held our special babies with their distended abdomen, green eyes and jaundiced skin yet looking so cute and special as we chatted on the challenges and hope we had for our challenged children. We put Dike and Azhar down to play for a while. Zaheera told me that her mother was in her early fifties and had come as a possible donor although she, Zaheera, was also the choice donor. Her husband was there to help with their other children, as well as be a minder to them when the surgeries were done. We wished each other well as I took Dike back to our room.

Dr. Neelam came to the room and I pleasantly told her that I had been with Dike to see my sister from South Africa. She quickly explained that in-house visits were not encouraged under the circumstances we found ourselves in. Also, considering that she had just spent one week to stabilize Dike, she did not think it would be to our advantage exposing him to another child with some other peculiar issues. Once more I learnt something new from Dr. Neelam.

As the days progressed, I had a better understanding of Dr. Neelam and her very high sense of values. As a paediatrician, she values her patients and puts their needs as priority. She dwells on perfection and has very little latitude for slackers. In her quick temper, she reprimands parents bluntly to take charge of their responsibilities if she finds they are out of tune with issues that are in the best interest of their predicament with their children. She always has genuine intentions and would always explain the reason for her reaction and occasional over reaction under certain situations. Her administrative skills were admirable and there was so much to learn from her. I had no doubt that God had led me to her. She simply believed that a parent had to take charge of the child's situation and be able to communicate all issues to enable the doctor take the best decision for the child.

On the day we were to be discharged, I had received a text message which bothered me. I would later talk to Dr. Neelam in the privacy of her office where she informed me that whilst with Zaheera earlier in the day, Zaheera had asked if it would be possible to donate parts of her liver to Dike as well as to her son. Dr. Neelam was so touched at the generosity of this woman who was truly a mother and willing to donate a part of her organ to another whom she barely knew. Dr. Neelam felt it was such an incredible gesture which I ought to hear to encourage me. I was so touched and once more I knew that help was on its way. I became overwhelmed with a new feeling of gratitude; an assurance once more that all would be well. I left Dr. Neelam's office in praise to God and gratitude for His great promises.

On the morning of the 25th of February 2009, Dr. Neelam came to the room to ask me to go look for an apartment to move into. Sweeti and Kanta had introduced to me a few housing agents. Dr. Neelam asked Sweeti to come to my room and baby sit Dike while I went house hunting. I was touched by her kind gestures.

Many of the apartments I saw were very regular by the Indian standard but were quite substandard by my reckoning; the rent was also not cheap. The property agent told me I had to pay three months in advance, make a security deposit and pay some other charges including his agency fee. I became upset for I thought they were ripping me off as a foreigner. After due consideration, I chose to go back to the hospital rather than make a hasty decision I might regret.

Later that day, some other doctors from other specialized units came for various assessments on Dike. I was so impressed with their team spirit and devotion to work.

At about midnight Delhi time, my aunt May called to encourage me and inform me that Ikolink, our family yahoo group, was upholding us that day in prayer and fasting. My aunt Adeline had called earlier in the day for an update on our situation and I informed her that Professor Egbonu had called the day before. As usual, I was glad to hear from my aunties and knew that I was not alone in the battle we faced. I was at peace in respect of my home, for I had Onyekachi Uduku and Chinenye Kalu, two ladies from The Everlasting

Covenant Parish who had moved into my home to take care of the children in Port-Harcourt. Sharon Adebola another friend from the same Parish whose younger children also went to Lead British International School dropped the children home daily after school. God sent us great help at our time of need and we remained grateful for these Ladies' sacrifice of love to us.

At the time we were about to be discharged from the hospital, I found out that our medical bill had not be paid. The money had been transferred to the hospital account from Nigeria but had not been received. As a result, we were not discharged on that day. The following day, the accounts department still had not yet received the money and Dr. Neelam later came to see me in respect of the report she had received from the billing section.

I explained to her that the bulk of the money for the transplant had been sent to the hospital account four days earlier but I was surprised the bank had not yet received it. She asked how much I owed the hospital and I said about $2,000 but I had a little over $1,800 with me. She asked how much I would need and I told her I would need about $300 to make up what I had and keep some change. Shortly after she left, she sent her secretary Kanta to cash a cheque and bring to me. I was grateful but felt dispirited for not being able to pay the bill promptly.

Eventually, I used all I had for the house rent to settle the hospital bill in addition to what Dr. Neelam lent me. The estate agent had also come that morning to tell me that the 28,000 rupees rent he told me a day earlier was just for one month. As I did not have that much money with me, I temporarily justified my decision to check into a hotel.

We were later discharged that evening and we moved into the Crystal Palace Hotel right opposite the hospital main entrance gate.

Weep Not

My days were always eventful; my spiritual routine was to read the Bible and the Open Heavens devotional before forging into the day. I always went back to the previous days' readings and it was usually mind blowing seeing the message in relation to the clear details of the day's activities; especially details of events I thought were insignificant and those I never visualised. These revelations which came in the quiet moments of my meditation would remain for me, the springboard I needed as confirmation on the purpose and mission on the lonesome sojourn in faraway India. I was totally in tune with the Lord who revealed so much to me and above all, gave me inner peace.

On Saturday the 28th of February 2009, I was woken by Iquo Emeni's phone call at about 3am. I fell asleep after we spoke, only to hear my phone ring again at 4.40am. This time it was Iquo's husband Ritchie, whose call came just as I awoke and about to change Dike. Ritchie told me he had come home late that night and his wife told him she had spoken to me. I was pleasantly surprised when he said he would not mind coming to India to donate his liver to save Dike. He had already spoken to Mike. Hearing this from him was mind blowing; these were the words of encouragement I needed at that very low moment of my life. I was totally overwhelmed with warmth for Ritchie and from that day onward, I regarded him as a brother.

There are people who would say something touching, emotional, encouraging and uplifting to the spirit. Being there, at the lowest ebb of my life, I found there were people who genuinely felt for us and were honestly willing to make the sacrifice to donate a part of their organ to save our son's life. These people, great men and women, had become my unsung everyday heroes.

I held onto God, my faith and hope. I believed in my affirmations and I had my swagger which was my outward appearance of an inward grace. Peace engulfed me and I picked up my pen and journal to make my entries for the day.

Again, as I reflected on the previous day's journal titled "Restorer of Joy", I read the memory verse which was Psalm 51:12:

> "Restore unto me the joy of thy salvation, and uphold me with thy free spirit."
> Psalm 51:12

Indeed, our God is the restorer of joy. Pastor Adeboye once wrote that one day at a supermarket with his children, while they chatted and cracked godly jokes, a white man who stood by shopping remarked, "your laughter makes me want to laugh".

The message was quite phenomenal for amid the confusion of the moment, the revelation would later prove to us that Jehovah Jireh would be the provider of our needs and the restorer of our joy as He simply and calmly urged me to *Weep Not*.

For Death Shall Not Hold Me Captive

As we faced the ordeal that befell my family, I watched the impact of fear and the inability to make concise decisions, knowing clearly that it was something we needed to deal with. Indecisiveness was enough to deal a heavy blow on us at that time. I reflected on the story of Abraham and Isaac and was convinced the best way was simply to obey the Lord in total submission to His will, for He would make the way for us or else the stress of indecision would deal with us. My song through those challenging times was:

> "My Soul shall magnify the Lord,
> And His Spirit shall fall over me,
> For death shall not hold me captive
> Even in the grave, Jesus is Lord
> Even in the grave, Jesus is Lord."

On one of those days in Rajinder Nager, my mum's first cousin Aunty Chidi Onwufor called. She encouraged me to remain faithful and hopeful for the Lord's intervention in Dike's situation. I agreed with her that miracles do happen and we were hopeful that the Lord had a purpose for Dike and I was sure we were already highly favoured.

On the 2nd of March 2009, Dike was in distress as he itched all through the night. He finally slept at 7am totally exhausted and yet he woke up at 10am. I gave him Ondansetron and then called Dr. Neelam to brief her of his ordeal. She prescribed Atarax, Ondansetron and Gardinal Syrup.

I had planned to pay for a house opposite the hospital which an agent had shown me the day before. Somehow, I developed cold feet and decided to forgo the house. I just could not think straight although it was a newly renovated two bedroom apartment on the ground floor of an old building. I was sceptical of rooming in the ground floor all alone with my little child. I felt I could get a better offer on the first floor of another building. I discussed the issue with Sylvia, Tonye's wife; she said since I was alone and going through so much physical, mental and emotional stress, she did not think it a great idea renting an apartment and being saddled with the responsibility of domestic chores.

I also discussed the housing issue with Sweeti who had been of great support to me. She advised against taking the house for if we had to move in on admission which could be anytime, it would mean a double billing to us. It was better to wait until we knew when the surgery was, and we were settled on so many other issues before renting an apartment. Their various opinions made much sense and I was grateful for their advice.

I believed that all things worked for the good of those that love God. Perhaps if I had taken that house, I would not have had the opportunity to explore New Delhi and gain all the knowledge and wisdom I acquired in the process. Knowing I would always have a cause to revisit India for medical checkups, business or for social visits, I gained the survival skills in the Pahar-Ganjh area, mingling and exploring different areas in search of housing, shopping for food from the local markets and also exploring the fabric business which would eventually sustain me in the few years thereafter.

While in the hotel however, hunger remained a major concern which eventually made me leave the Crystal Palace Hotel in search of a hotel where I could cook my own food.

I expected Mike to arrive in India that morning but his trip was cancelled. As we went through the challenges that faced us, Sweeti turned out to be as sweet as her name. She would send me daily spirit lifting text messages to encourage me. We usually had our consultations with Dr. Neelam every four days and Preeti was very pleasant to us each time we came.

Over the next few days, Mike called a few times and also sent me series of text messages asking that I forgive his shortcomings. I became very emotional for I knew he was hurting as much as I was, if not even more. I understood he was worried but I wished he could communicate his fears and worries to me; unfortunately we weren't being expressive to each other and this was actually causing us great stress. I decided to remain calm. Dike's challenge was not stressing me as much as the emotional challenge Mike and I were going through, but I trusted that the Lord would see us through. I completely understood his fears – our fears - although I was often upset that perhaps he did not believe that I understood how he felt. I knew we would overcome with time.

"Perhaps we will someday have a cause to help raise awareness over medical challenges back home in Nigeria;" I thought to myself. I called those periods 'The Dark Ages in our Lives'".

Those were the words I wrote in my journal that day. The lack of emotional support during such challenging times was another main area of future focus, especially for people who faced similar health challenges. In more developed nations, caregivers and support groups were usually available to give emotional support to the very sick and also their families but in my country Nigeria, such groups were hard to find. Although there were many non-governmental agencies (NGOs) and foundations set up for various purposes, none was known to be available for those suffering from liver and ancillary diseases. The church, families, friends or acquaintances were usually the option for such emotional support. As many of the people had little or no experience regarding the depth of the medical challenges, most patients ended up with advice based on limitations and ignorance.

From what we had been through, we found that the doctors were also never generous with information, so most patients resorted to prayers or visiting prayer houses. Some would even go for local or herbal treatments or worse still, they would patronise native doctors and juju priests. Unfortunately, issues that required a little medical solution ended up as matters of spiritual warfare.

Although I was saddened by the fact that the paediatric doctors I had met in Nigeria did not know of many hospitals outside Nigeria to refer their patients, I was glad we got a referral to India. There have been several medical breakthroughs in liver transplantation from 2001 till date by the renowned liver transplant pioneer, Dr. Avinder Singh Soin, and his team. Dr. Soin is recognized all over the world for his pioneering work in liver transplantation with a success rate of 90-95%.

In Nigeria, liver diseases and some other ailments are still seen as death sentences. I am saddened when I recollect how a close medical doctor friend of ours had told us when we returned from our first trip to India with Dike, that we had done all that we needed to do for our son Dike. I was angry for a very long time for his ignorant opinion.

I did not believe the negative and could not wait to see the ray of light at the end of the tunnel which I knew would come at the appointed time.

Having seen the effect of fear on decision making, I already knew I had to remain steadfast on the right path. I knew that fear could paralyse one into not taking the right decision at the right time or even not take any decision at all. We had seen the consequence of this which we paid for dearly when we had delayed reacting to Dr. V.S.S's advice that we plan our return to India within six months of our first trip. He stated that the medications were temporary measures whose efficacy would possibly last for about six months. We started noticing the change in Dike during the fifth month when he began to itch again, which signified the beginning of the end stage of the liver disease.

The outpouring of love towards us was heart-warming. On Sunday the 1st of March 2009, I received a call from Chief Mrs. Veronica Ajuebon, my children's proprietress in Port-Harcourt. During our conversation, she kept saying "Dike will be well" and I should be wise in my dealings and in my thinking. She also encouraged me to keep my faith. I also received a call from Mike's cousin Zuby who lives in Seattle, Washington. We spoke for over an hour and he praised me for my courage. He said I was already doing what I knew best to do in order to save my son.

In The Heart Of Delhi

On the day of my next visit to Dr Neelam, I ran into two Nigerian women; Cecilia Iwuofor and her younger sister, Akudo. They asked about my welfare and wondered how I was coping. I told them it was a big challenge especially as I had difficulty in communicating effectively with Indians. They understood my plight and said they would help; I was curious to know what they could do to assist me. Cecilia took me to the very busy district of Pahar Ganjh which was about five kilometres away from Rajinder Nager. She negotiated a hotel for me that would enable me cook in my room. It was even at a cheaper room rate than where I stayed. She said she would renegotiate with them for a lower rate on the premise that I would stay for three months. I had to buy an electric cooker and couldn't wait to cook my own food.

Pahar Ganjh reminded me of the ever busy Obalende, Ojuelegba and the Ikeja bus stop areas in Lagos. It seemed an unpleasant neighbourhood with all kinds of people and various activities going on; I wondered why I had to go a place like that with Cecilia. But

I needed to eat and Dr. Neelam had advised me to cook certain meals for Dike which I could not do in any of the hotels around the Hospital. As we walked around, I realised that even in that somewhat squalid environment, there was a huge population of foreign tourists who were lodged in the hotels that littered the area. They were in the cybercafés, the cafés, the Western Union offices and the restaurants. As my eyes opened, I realised there was probably more to that neighbourhood than met the eyes.

Cecelia took me to a restaurant called Malhotra and advised me to dine there if I was hungry. I went back to Rajinder Nager, moved my belongings to the Sruya Place Hotel and went for dinner at the Malhotra restaurant. I was pleasantly surprised to find I was the only black there. Everyone else was Caucasian. I thoroughly enjoyed my meal and returned to the hotel, cleaned the room and fell asleep at 2am.

Three days later, Cecelia took me to the INA market about 40 minutes away. The locals and the Nigerians call it the Ayeni Market which sounds Yoruba. I was glad she took me to the market to purchase all I needed for a comfortable stay in the confines of my hotel room.

On Friday, I took Dike who had frequent stools, to see Dr. Neelam. As we waited, he relieved himself all over me. After we had cleaned up, we went in to see Dr. Neelam. I was touched by her carriage, grace and charisma. She saw us briefly for she had so many patients waiting. While with her, I finally met the family that had been in the media for the first Domino transplant. I spoke to one of the mothers while Dr. Neelam hurriedly left us for the airport. She would later text me from the airport to apologize for the little attention she gave us. In her message she wrote that she was very sad at what was going on in respect of Dike's issues but assured me that she would do everything she could to save him. She said she loves us and would miss us. While reaffirming her belief that I have a good aura, she said I should trust her to do her very best for us.

What more could I hope to hear from my baby's doctor? I was so touched and totally won over by her openness. I knew I could trust her with Dike.

Dr. Neelam sent me many more text messages as the months progressed. She was a very caring doctor who was thorough and had no threshold for lapses from her staff, aides, and team of doctors or from the numerous parents of her paediatric patients. She became my mentor in my sojourn. I saw a totally committed doctor, mother and friend as I watched and learnt from her. Her work schedule and work ethics were incredible as I had seen her in hospital performing endoscopic procedures on her patients as early as 7am daily.

She would do her ward rounds before consulting from 2pm till about 4pm Mondays through Saturdays seeing a minimum of 50 patients at each stretch. I had bumped into her in different rooms in the hospital at odd times performing one official procedure or consultation between the hours of 10am and 2pm, and also between 4pm and 6pm, if she was not in the wards attending to her patients, or brainstorming for the best solutions possible with her team of liver specialists and interns.

She was quick tempered, and I often saw her frown when parents of patients were slow in communicating relevant information she required to make her diagnosis, prescription or advice. She expected everyone to be coherent and forthcoming with information and she was always quick to tell parents that she is the doctor but for her to help, they needed to give her all the details as fast as she asked to enable her take quick decisions. Most of the children she saw were already in critical conditions having been diagnosed elsewhere and then brought to her for further treatment/ solution therefore she was always focused in her approach to minimise time wastage and get the best solutions as fast as she and her team could. With her, I understood why their success rate for liver transplantation was very high.

On a day that was surgery free, she would leave the hospital at about 6pm; she lived about an hour's drive from the hospital. She would do consultations in her home before retiring for the day at past midnight. Most of the text messages she sent me were at midnight when she had unwound for the day. Sometimes, she would send a message to tell me about a patient she was worried about or to enquire about Dike's condition. It was almost impossible to exchange pleasantries in her consulting room for she was thoroughly professional at work. Occasionally, she would send a message saying she could not sleep because she was worried about Dike as she had vowed to save him. We would exchange about three or four messages at midnight before we finally said our goodnights.

Dr. Neelam was simply incredible and I had no doubt in my mind that the LORD would use her mightily for Dike's testimony. One day, Dr. Neelam sent me a text message that read thus:

> "Trust me honey, I want to do my best to save Dike, both of you are amazing people. I feel you have an aura which makes me feel good."

And in another text, she wrote:

> "I really hope God takes out an alternative for I keep
> thinking of
> Dike and you."

Replying her message, I wrote how I felt truly blessed to have met her and having her as Dike's doctor and consultant, and how I was truly awed by her passion especially towards Dike. I told her that she had truly found her calling and the Lord would continue to bless her for the numerous children she strives to save.

We continued with our consultations with Dr. Neelam every four days and each time we saw her, she hoped we would find a solution for Dike. We knew it was not possible to find a donor who was not a blood relation. She had her doubts about being able to help me find a solution for a liver donor for Dike. She acknowledged that I stood on faith and was very strong as we consistently interacted. Eventually she started seeing herself as the help God had directed us to for Dike's breakthrough because I had consistently told her so.

As she also continued to hope and pray for a solution for any of our family members with a suitable blood group and healthy liver to come forth to save Dike, she had a sudden flash in her brain on what to do. The revelation was what eventually led to a phenomenal decision that made all the difference in our state of affairs. She had a flash in her brain that since I had been willing to donate a part of my liver to save my son, then it could be possible to find help among the hundreds of patients she held consultations with weekly.

The help however would be in the form of a swap whereby that other patient who did not have a suitable donor could trade places with me as donor; if that patient's unsuitable donor would be a match for my son.

Dr. Neelam's revelation had been at her finger tips yet she nor anyone around her had not been able to analyse the possibility until that particular moment when she had that flash in her brain.

The following day, as I walked into her consulting room, in excitement, she told me she had finally thought out a possible solution for Dike. She did not tell me what the solution was but on another day she asked me to be patient for about a month for she was convinced she would find a solution for Dike because of the number of patients she saw daily. She always emphasized that I kept our wishes and thoughts to myself.

Our stay in India gave me time to reflect. I pondered on what I could learn or do to add value to my life. I knew I wanted to do something positive with myself but since I was nursing a child, it was difficult to do anything engaging. Dike stooled very frequently, his bum was usually red, irritatingly painful and needed constant exposure. He was fed frequently too as he could not digest his food properly. He had diarrhoea very often and had to be changed frequently, sometime up to 20 times in a day. For him to have lived like that and survived for 18 months was indeed a miracle. Despite all those challenges, Dike remained physically strong.

I could not do so much with him under my sole care so, I spent my time reading books and writing excerpts in my journal.

Meanwhile, Dike remained very strong and active, and I thought to myself with a smile, "boys will always be boys". To my mortification, Dike began to roll off the low hotel bed. The day he fell face down on the cold hotel floor, without further ado, I asked the hotel receptionist where I could get a cot. I was directed to Rajori Garden where there were a number of malls. We took the sub-way to the mall. I got a lovely cot and a beetle baby walker and Dike seemed very pleased with his new possessions because he kept smiling a lot.

Thursday the 12th of March 2009 was Dr. Neelam's birthday; it was also the Indian festival of Dolyatra which is usually a public holiday celebrated to send away evil and usher in the good. All over the country, people played with colours and had carnivals on the streets. I sent a text to Dr. Neelam at past midnight to wish her a happy birthday and to my surprise, she replied promptly. She said she had a party in her home and the last guest had just left at about 1am.

The next day, we went to consult with Dr. Neelam. Dike had become very itchy again, and she asked me to wait for her office assistant to type a letter to accompany the slide they were forwarding to a laboratory in the United Kingdom for analysis. It was 4pm. While waiting in the reception, Dike and I fell asleep. I woke up surprised to find the reception hall was empty. I looked at my watch and it was 6.35pm. I quickly called Sweetie and she told me she was on her way home but I should go to the next room and see if Maam was still there. I went in and found her with her male assistant, Gurov. She was surprised to see me and she offered me the last piece of her cake and told me she had bought food for her team but they ate all and even forgot to offer her some.

After I left her, I went to the bank to confirm if the money we sent to the hospital through my brother had been received. They eventually confirmed receipt of the $25,000 USD for Dike's bill which had been sent on the 27th of February 2009. Although the money had reached the bank on the 3rd of March 2009, it had been difficult to trace because my brother's name appeared in the system instead of Dike's. Mike called me that evening and I told him I had met other liver transplant patients and their donors who had come for check-up. Once again, Mike battled with his emotions and it hurt me to hear the pain in his voice. He had spoken to my uncle Agunze who later called me and was happy to hear I was okay and handling the challenge as best as I could, and cheerfully too.

I had long realised that God's gifts are not always perfect but we have to remain grateful and find happiness no matter how difficult the situation was.

Dike had slept from 8pm till 12am. He was awake till we both fell asleep at about 4am and after just two hours, we woke again at 6am to feed. That done, we slept till 9am before finally rising to start our day.

On our next visit to Dr. Neelam, she asked me to do another CT scan which would give more details of my internal organs specifically the liver. It cost Rs 8,500 which then was about a hundred and fifty U.S dollars. She informed me that she had spoken to a family in respect of the solution she had thought of for Dike and asked that we keep our fingers crossed. She said she had to prepare me for the possibility of donating part of my liver as she goes ahead with the rest of the work-up on me.

As I read "When He Touches" in the Open Heavens devotional for Friday 13th of March 2009, it ministered to me on Dr. Neelam's divine involvement in our affairs, especially her text messages of hope. Divine involvement means God having a hand in something. In Mark 1: 40-45, a leper met Jesus and asked if He was willing to heal him. Jesus was first filled with compassion before healing him, and this was the Lord's way of saying, "Not only will I heal you but from now on I want to have a hand in your affairs".

If an Indian woman of the Hindu religion can have a hand in our affairs even as we were foreigners and sojourners in her country, how much more our Lord and Saviour Jesus Christ, who in the scriptures promised us healing and divine health? The devotional reminded me of the Bible passage on healing in 1 Peter 2: 24.

> "Who his own self bare our sins in his own body on the tree that we, being dead to sin, should live unto righteousness by whose stripes we were healed."
> 1 Peter 2: 24

On Monday the 16th of March, I had a very heavy heart. Dr. Neelam had informed me that our plan was proving very difficult due to government regulations. She was sad as she looked at Dike's test results with his bilirubin of over 20u/moL/L and albumin at a 2.3g/L low count, her worry being that Dike was at the end stage of the disease and she knew what that meant but she also knew there was still a chance to do something positive if a donor emerged.

Once more I was touched when I heard her mutter a prayer, "Oh God! Please which angel will come and save this baby now?"

Her worries become contagious but we kept on praying and believing God. I had no doubt that my God would deliver Dike from the affliction despite the doctor's report. Dr. Neelam knew we stood on faith, and part of my prayer was that the Indian doctors would experience the mercy of God on Dike and they will acknowledge that indeed the Lord we serve was able to deliver him. I also knew that even if the end result was not as desired, our God will still be Lord, as the three Hebrew boys spoke in Daniel 3:17 when King Nebuchadnezzar ordered they be thrown into the burning furnace for refusing to bow and worship his image.

I was still receiving phone calls and encouragement from my family and friends. My Aunt May called from Abuja and cousin Ify called from New York. Later, cousin Ucheora called me from Washington D.C. and we talked about the family challenges. He advised me to get someone to stay with me and render some physical support. I told him Aunty Adeline was planning to come in another month or so. He was concerned about Mike and felt he would need support too from men he could listen to, for he was going through a lot of trauma as well. I was glad he called.

I was exhausted after I spoke to my relations and to Mike, so I decided to put off my phone to silence all calls. Before I could, I saw the phone beep and it was Mrs. Ajuebon; I was glad to take her call. I cried as we spoke despite my inner strength which apparently at that point was hanging on a threshold for it was a most trying period for me as I battled with so many issues.

She scolded me, asking where my faith was. She was compassionate and encouraged me to have faith that all will be well. She said I was weeping like one who had no faith. She asked for Mike's number which I forwarded to her as we ended our conversation.

After we spoke, I found it very difficult to sleep so I called Mike's brother in Kaduna. I apologized for our long absence since Christmas and having not properly briefed him as an elder in the family on the situation we faced. I told him also that I respect my husband's privacy which was the main reason for not updating him on Dike's situation and he confessed to being terrified especially after Mike had briefed him in December about Dike's condition. He said he would talk to Mike after I had allayed his fears about the situation for the proposed transplant.

I later spoke to my Aunt May who said she and her siblings, Dr. Nwosu and Agunze, had spoken to Mike. They had advised him that it was better we stayed together and encourage each other since we were going through so much. Afterwards, cousin Dike called and was of the same opinion. Anyi, Tonye and Dike had shown much concern over the recent development; although I was far away from them I could imagine their concern knowing I was going through so much to save my only son. All I needed was the emotional support and this helped knowing that our families, friends and the church were constantly praying for us.

I continued to encourage Mike to let go of his fear and worries for all would be well. I encouraged him to hold on to faith; we were in this together. I had read a lot of scripture and the ministrations through the phone calls also helped my faith, especially after Mrs. Ajuebon had asked "where was my faith?"

The confirmation of this came in the Open Heavens reading of 17th of March 2008, titled "Satan Detests Faith" with the text taken from Hebrews 10: 23,

> "Let us hold fast the profession of our faith without wavering" (for he is faithful that promised)."
> Hebrews 10: 23

Every time I got those confirmations from my daily scripture readings, I became stronger and more peaceful despite the turmoil in my heart; they were confirmations that God was involved with what we were dealing with. I knew He carried me when I thought my legs were no longer strong to walk and feel. These incidents were not mere coincidences, but destiny being fulfilled in my life and for the little boy whom God had sent to the world through us.

Pastor Adeboye taught that Satan hates anyone who steps out in faith and is always ready to do anything possible to make such a person give up. What you see either feeds your faith or fuels your fear. Therefore, we are urged to take our gaze off anything capable of breeding fear in us but to feed our eyes with what feeds faith. When Peter was sinking, he cried out to the Lord for help and he was saved; we should do likewise when in need.

I cried out to the Lord in my distress and He brought comfort to my soul. Before the end of the day, I received a text message from my uncle Agunze. He said that he had spoken with Mike and he planned to be in India the following Wednesday.

Brother Act - The Mediator

My brother Tonye called a few days later and we had a very deep conversation. He said he had a chat with Mike, and he had spoken about his fears. Tonye told me Mike's fears are real, however he was convinced that Dike's challenge was for a reason - to bring Mike and I closer to God. He said Mike's biggest fear was how I would be able to fend for the family if something went wrong with the surgery should he decide to donate his liver. He was still in pain from the surgery he had, his mother was also a challenging geriatric in his sole care. His business, which was the main source of our finances, and so many other issues caused him anxiety. To hear this was heart wrenching.

Tonye was full of meaningful advice and I listened attentively. He said that since Mike had opened up to the things that caused him anxiety the most, we should seize the opportunity to address certain issues; we should take the outcome in good faith for it would bring about good dividends in our marriage if handled well. He then asked if we had any form of life insurance, a will, if we had made plans about our future and other such issues that when discussed and sorted, will enable one take risks in life with peace of mind. He told me that people are usually scared of death when they have not planned their exit from this world and unfortunately, most people never really plan this, rather they perceive death as morbid instead of an honourable transition.

I repeatedly sang "For death shall not hold me captive, even in the grave, Jesus is Lord".

Coping With The Medical Challenge

By Thursday the 26th of March 2009, having waited so long, I was totally surrendered to God. Dike, was still suffering from the diarrhoea he had developed 20 days earlier and the last ten days were so bad that all I did was clean up after the endless mess. His buttocks were so sore and I hardly used diapers for it worsened his situation. I only resorted to the use of diapers when I was exhausted and needed a break from the constant cleaning.

Eventually, Dr. Neelam advised me to use Eumosone cream, T-bact oil and Siloderm cream. I was to mix all on my palm and then rub on his buttocks and groin region. This worked like magic and I was so relieved.

Five days earlier, Dike had lost his appetite and I forced him to drink his medication. The doctor had prescribed a medication for me to stop lactating and the day I had planned to take that medication turned out to be the day that Dike lost his appetite for food, so I continued to breast feed him and that soothed him. He was only able to take two bottles of milk with Protinex daily which was not much. He would drink some water but I often forced him to take ORS. He had developed a fever and once more had been placed on twelve different medications including Questrain, with one third of a pack three times daily. I just could not wait to see him stop at least half of those medications.

As I ate lunch on one of those days, Dike managed to eat a few slices of banana and I was so excited. On Thursday the 26th of March 2009 he said "bye-bye" as he waved; I was ecstatic. Dike was starting to talk! That night, he climbed down from the bed while I was in the bathroom. Despite his ill health, he was truly amazing.

CHAPTER 5

Hope With The Jhejani Couple

On Saturday morning, the 28th of March 2009, Mike finally arrived Delhi. I arranged for a car to pick him up.

We went to see Doctor Neelam on Tuesday and she welcomed Mike. After her consultations with Dike, she asked Mike to run some tests but asked me to see her later on Wednesday. On Thursday, Mike and I went back to see her and she said she had news for a possible swap. A family had come from another part of the country and the woman would require a donor like we did. Her husband could be a possible donor to Dike but would not be able to donate to his wife. The doctors thought of the possibility of swapping with us. Doctor Neelam had briefed me alone on Wednesday as she deemed it best to speak with me before breaking the news to Mike whom she had never met, except through their initial communication months before I met her. After she gave us the information, she told us to find a quiet place and discuss it.

It was an agonising discussion and I felt Mike had a lot of mixed feelings; I tried to convince him it was okay by me. We had gone through so much stress and I was very relieved that for the first time, he had proof that the doctors had no intention of pressurizing him to be a donor. His biggest shock was the fact that I was willing to be a donor. His first instinct was a rejection of the suggestion, but I quickly told him that it is my body and I was mentally and physically fit to go through it to save our son. He was dumbfounded and I knew a lot of thoughts were going through his mind. He had gone through several harrowing experiences.

There was the robbery incident in our early marriage that left him almost dead, followed by the series of surgeries he had undergone to remove the numerous pellets lodged in his upper and lower arm, more especially the more recent surgery which still left him in pain. I remembered his witnessing Dike's birth, which was my fourth caesarean section and the only birthing of our four children he witnessed, and it had left him mesmerized for weeks.

He had come into the delivery room with a camera to video the procedures but by the time he saw the incision, the blood and the flesh, he was awed. The doctors told him to go ahead and film the delivery. He was so shaken and could not do much with the camera but kept walking in and out of the theatre in panic. For the rest of the week he continued to exclaim that indeed women are great, very strong and unique beings. And here we were once again to face another procedure.

Dr. Neelam ran more tests on me from that Thursday evening until Sunday, as Friday was a public holiday. She had planned to go on a brief vacation in two weeks and wanted all tests collated before meeting with the Organ Donor Committee, which was to sit on the 8th of April 2009. At that time she was concerned about Dike who was in total distress and at the mercy of God. She knew that the sooner the surgery was done the better for him but she also needed her vacation for she had worked extremely hard and usually had little time for her family.

She wanted the surgery done as soon as possible to give her at least five days to monitor Dike's progress before she left town. The next committee would meet on the 22nd of April 2009 and she felt that was almost a month away and too far. The days moved fast.

We had planned to go to the Nigerian Embassy on the 7th of April 2009, which was also anniversary of my late mother's passing, but the day was declared a public holiday again by the Indian government. It was mandatory that we got a clearance letter from our country's Embassy in addition to some legal letters from a Notary Public. We could not go to the Embassy until the next day which was the same day the committee was sitting. The Committee was to sit at 4pm, so we had to leave early in the morning to be back before they sat. Our outing included picking up reports from the anaesthesiologist, gynaecologist and pathologist, and lastly, the report at Dr. Soin's office.

It was a major challenge at the hospital which then was planning its 100th year anniversary; a lot of restructuring was being done as well as some massive renovations. The units were disjointed so there was so much ground to cover picking up reports from the different departments. Although there were elevators, they usually had long queue and only the very ill patients and elderly were given preference. The waiting areas were also very busy and the few available seats were usually occupied by the very sick and elderly patients, therefore a day's trip to the hospital usually left one very exhausted.

As we progressed with our plan, we were also making plans for my aunt Adeline to come stay with us. I got Dr. Neelam's secretary to prepare a letter to the Indian High Commission in Nigeria for my Aunt's visa.

In the Open Heavens devotional for 8th of April 2009, the message was titled "Part This Red Sea" with the text taken from Exodus 14: 15-16.

> "And the Lord said unto Moses" wherefore criest thou unto me? Speak unto the children of Israel that they go forward: but lift thou up the rod, and stretch out thine hand over the sea and divide it; and the children of Israel shall go on dry ground through the midst of the sea.
> Exodus 14: 15-16

After I read this text, I was convinced that I was treading on the right path with my decision. Very often Mike would say let God's will be done concerning Dike and I always agreed with him, backing up our belief with scriptures. My justification remained that God would always give a confirmation text through the Open Heavens devotional.

I take time to explain these issues not because I am righteous, but to encourage the readers of my book that there is divine revelation through the scriptures and that if we have spiritual eyes, then we will have peace whilst going through certain challenges of life.

My belief was backed up by the revelation of this text titled "Part This Red Sea". Man's will is usually done but God backs it up as only He, The Almighty has the final say. In the commentary, Pastor Adeboye stated that it was not really God that parted the Red Sea but Moses, for God asked him to stretch out his rod. He obeyed, so God backed him up. If he had disobeyed the Lord, that would have been his choice and then the Red Sea would not have parted.

I had also reflected and discussed the story of Abraham and God's instruction to him to sacrifice his only son Isaac. Abraham had a choice to obey or to disobey. He chose the former and God provided the ram. If he had disobeyed, then he would not have been called a friend of God and he would have missed out on all the blessings God had in store for him.

The Open Heaven devotional says the Red Sea could denote a common problem affecting everyone under a particular leader, congregation or family. As parents, have you parted the Red Sea that could hinder your children's glorious future? If you do not do it, God will not do it for you. "Until you part the Red Sea before you, heaven will keep looking on passively".

I believed this was Dike's predicament, therefore I knew I had to take the decision to part the Red Sea in our lives, and then wait for the miracle to happen.

Diaries Of The Heart

We were in the heart of Delhi, it had been a stressful day out and I returned to the apartment exhausted. I dozed off for about twenty minutes then my phone rang. It was my aunty Adeline calling to tell me she was concerned about discussing me with her sisters. They felt I was not communicating and had heard that I wanted to donate my liver. I told her to discuss with them if she wanted but I still chose to be silent because I did not need any distraction at that point in time.

I felt that my affair should not be subjected to a debate. It was strictly my business and I was ready for whatever the outcome may be. I just needed their moral support as a family, especially through prayers.

After my conversation with my aunt, Mike and I talked into the night and he said perhaps something good will come out of this challenge we faced. He said he was very proud of me and maybe a Foundation or NGO would be birthed after the experience. I felt great hearing this from my dear husband and I knew it was proof that for this great cause, the Lord would endorse it and it would be our take home package from India.

As Mike and I talked that night, I asked him if it was a coincidence that Dike was born looking like a little Indian boy and we chose to call him Nadim.

Delay Is Not Denial

We were under a lot of pressure to complete the legal work before meeting with the committee. Cecilia had hired a cab to take us to a court to get the affidavit which cost us about Rs.3000, and we hurried back to the hospital in time for the committee's convening. Unfortunately, we did not meet the deadline for while our own documents were complete, the couple Kiran Jhejani and her husband, were not ready with their medical reports. We could not meet up with the committee requirements and I become very weepy. When I consulted with Dr. Neelam and seeing that I was fretting, she quickly told me to calm down stating that the medical team were still sorting the Jhejani family medical records, so I should relax till the next committee meeting in two weeks.

I had reasons to worry. Dike's condition was deteriorating and we all knew it. Secondly, Mike was already with us in anticipation of the surgery and would soon have to return to our children in Abuja and to his business in Port Harcourt. He still needed to work to enable the bills be paid therefore any extension of his time in Delhi meant loss of revenue to the family and his business, and the bills just needed to be paid. The third reason was that Dr. Neelam was already booked to travel overseas and had said she wanted the surgery done at least five days prior to her departure so she would physically monitor Dike in his first few days in intensive care.

We had no choice but to relax and get all documentation ready. All was in God's perfect will for us. We went to the very busy High Court in the heart of Delhi to find a lawyer to do an affidavit, only to have it rejected by Dr. Sukchitra, the doctor who handled the paper-work for the transplant committee. We later had to go with the Jhejani family to another part of Delhi to get another affidavit for the sum of Rs.500. We could not believe it cost so little having paid so much a day earlier. We then went with the Jhejanis to the Indian Magistrates' court to get their clearance report, before we went back to the Nigerian Embassy to get another letter stating that the doctors' plan was for a swap transplant with the Jhejani couple, and not me donating to Dike as the first letter stated. What a hectic day.

As the weeks progressed slowly, we had to do some blood tests for DNA reports to establish the relationship of the donor to the recipient before we finally went for the committee screening. The members of the committee were the Board of the hospital, the government representatives, the surgeons and a few members of the medical team. The primary aim of the committee was to ensure they interviewed the patients and the donors and to establish their fitness to undergo the surgery.

They needed to be sure the donors were doing so out of their own volition. Donors had to be emotionally fit and willing to donate without any financial or material gain that could result in litigation, which could land the doctors in jail or to lose their license. The hospital needed to be sure of the documentation as it was a high risk surgery for both the patient and the donor, and also for the reputation of the hospital.

A DNA test, therefore, is usually required and if there were no blood ties, there had to be reasonable proof that there existed strong family relationships such as a step-father, step-mother, foster parentage or adopted relationships, or perhaps a best friend.

We needed the DNA proof that I am Dike's mother, while the Jhejani's did their tests and provided an affidavit and marriage certificate as proof of their conjugal relationship. We were cleared by the committee and the doctors fixed the date of surgery for the 22nd of May 2009. We were told we would be admitted two days before the surgery.

Meeting with the Jhejani's left me with some reservations despite the fact that we had no choice. My instinct was contrary to what the doctors hoped to achieve; I could feel it having interacted with them for the two weeks prior to the committee's sitting. We were under duress but I kept up with my faith that God's will be done concerning the swap. Mr. Jhejani was stocky, heavily built and in his mid-fifties. He had a lot of questions to ask about the transplant and did not quite seem to have made up his mind to go through with it.

At our second encounter with the couple, Khiran, who was also in her fifties, told me she would be happy if I gave up eating beef for her sake because she did not eat it as a result of her religion. I found that request very strange and I asked God for a revelation concerning that. I believed that if one were in dire need of something, especially with the type of challenge both our families were faced with, the last thing to worry about would be what the donor ate.

We would eventually wait till the 30th of April as we expected a call from the surgeon's office requesting us to come for admission into hospital. The phone call did not come and we called the office only to be told to meet with Dr. Soin on the 2nd of May 2009 for a briefing on some new developments.

The Open Heavens devotional message for the 30th of April 2009 was titled "One More Hour" with text taken from 2 Kings 13:14-19. It stated that those who faint hardly ever overcome problems, for when they are so close to their miracles, they give up. In the commentary, we were advised by Pastor Adeboye not to give up on anything we had laid our hands on that year, for we would reach our goal since our efforts in our prayers were not in vain. The message was very appropriate for how we felt at that time.

That Saturday, 2nd of May 2009 was the proposed date for our surgeries. Mike and I went to see Dr. Soin and he briefed us that the surgery was called off after they saw the MRI and other reports of Mr. Maresh Jhejani. He explained in depth the intricate details of matching an organ from recipient to donor. He said I had a good liver for Khiran as my blood and her blood were both A^+. On the other hand, Mr. Jhejani whose B+ blood group matched Dike's, had a very fatty liver and was not considered a good fit. Dr. Soin went further to explain the intricate details in the best way he could communicate to us.

He said that Dike's body weight was less than 12kg and he would need a piece of liver of about 100 grams to fit, and this piece would have to be cut to the right venation. The tail portion of Mr. Jhejani's left liver lobe if cut would weight about 400 grams, and that would not be a good match therefore would be too great a risk to take. He further said that his team of doctors were thorough and usually worked with 95% confidence level. He explained that doing otherwise would be like putting a round peg in a square hole. There would be bile leaks and a lot of complications would set in as the liver was a very delicate organ, which made the surgery a very risky one.

"Why would anyone then attempt using an organ that is not best fit and then endanger both lives?" asked Dr. Soin.

He emphasized that the ultimate aim was to save lives and not to risk or endanger life that was already going through several challenges, including the risk of losing all the money paid in multiples of thousands of dollars.

As Dr. Soin spoke, one thing became certain in Mike's mind which he later confessed to me. That first day encounter so impression Mike and he knew he could trust Dr. Soin for his thoughtfulness and thoroughness in handling his patients and their families. It was very clear from Dr. Soin's explanation and his body language that the doctors were not interested merely in taking their patients' money nor in the number of liver transplant cases they undertook, but about the safety of their surgical procedures and in the number of lives they saved.

Dr. Soin explained that his team were always certain that the donors did not have much to worry about, but the recipient who would still have a lot of challenges after the surgeries, were the ones to worry about. When he had exhausted all he had to say to us, Mike asked that he be considered as the donor, but Dr. Soin declined for he did not think Mike's liver was right for Dike and he also did not want to deal with any emotional instability for he was already on the path to finding an alternative for the swap.

When Mike insisted, the surgeon said he would ask for his MRI scan to check the details of his liver. He still did not think it would be a good option but he needed the benefit of doubt. Dr. Soin wrote the request for the MRI and asked us to have that done and come back to him with the report in a couple of days.

Years later as I edited my writings, my attention was drawn to the Open Heavens devotional message of 2nd of April 2009, the day Dr. Neelam informed us about Maresh and Khiran Jhejhani. Heaven had already recorded that we were not the right match with the Jhejanis. The title of the message was "Double Losers" with text taken from Jude 5–7. This was very thought provoking as it recounted the story of Lot's wife who, despite being spared with her family through the intercession from her uncle-in-law, Abraham, she still lost her life.

We returned to see Dr Soin on the afternoon of Monday the 4th of May 2009 with the MRI report, and as soon as he saw the film he said he knew Mike would not be a good match. The details revealed that while Dike needed about 100 grams of liver, that portion of Mike's liver when cut would weight about 350 grams, therefore was not the best fit.

Dr. Soin gave us an assurance of hope about a couple from Mumbai who had just arrived Delhi. The wife Priya needed a liver transplant as a result of Hepatitis C infection. Her husband being very slim would be the best solution, if all his tests came out right. He could donate to Dike while I donate to Priya. The tentative date for surgery was already fixed for the 10th of May 2009. We felt relieved and thankful to God as we left Dr. Soin's office hoping for the glimmer of light in our darkest moments.

Later that day, I saw Dr. Neelam after my blood sample was taken. She had requested I re-run some of the tests I had earlier done. She was convinced that I was very fit to donate my liver but she had to place me on an expensive medication called Valcyte which I had to take for about one month, prior to the surgery. She said it was necessary to take that medication so Priya Ahuja's body would be able to receive my liver without any antigen in me working to destroy her own system. The cost of Valcyte then was Rs550 per tablet which then was $10.00 and I had to take one and a half tablets every day amounting to $450 for the one month of consumption.

I had a lot of respect for Dr. Neelam for I saw the effort she and her team made towards continuous research in their field. Despite the fact that she knew I was very fit to donate to Priya she still felt she needed to discuss her findings in my blood report with her professional colleagues at a world convention for liver specialists which she was scheduled to attend in Europe that week.

As the days progressed, we waited for the hospital to call us for admission a day before the due date. Once again, just like with the Jhejani's, in our anxiety we called Dr. Soin's office and his secretary asked us to come see the surgeon. Again Dr. Soin apologized for the new development, explaining that Mrs. Ahuja had developed some lymph nodules on her neck and they suspected she was incubating tuberculosis in her body which is usually common with the type of ailment she was suffering from.

They were going to run tests on her to confirm this and if indeed it was tuberculosis, then she would be treated for six weeks. This was the minimum time frame for tuberculosis treatment and if she pulled through, then the surgery would be planned. However, at that time Dike was also struggling with the end stage of liver cirrhosis and they did not know if he had six weeks of grace. I told the doctor that Dike would hang in there for he was already a testimony. I said that if God could keep him that long and if the donor option had already manifested, then I was so sure that God will perfect His plan and purpose for the child.

For every positive affirmation I made, the doctors agreed that I had 'great faith; for Dike was suffering from biliary atresia which usually did not give its victim one year grace. Dike was one year and five months old and despite his being at the end stage of the disease, he had incredible strength. Each test we did came out worse than the previous, so metabolically, his body was degenerating but physically he was gaining strength. That was the Spirit of God in action supplying the daily miracles. Dike was not walking yet but he usually crawled round the apartment and held objects to walk around. In our apartment, there was a wooden rectangular coffee table which was quite heavy, but in his euphoria when he was not itching all over, Dike would push the table round the living room, which was an incredible feat I witnessed daily and that strengthened my faith. Each time he pushed the table, I would hear a voice ask me, "look at him, does he look like he is dying?" Then I would reflect on the promises of the Lord and read once more my earlier writings on "whose report will you believe?" With all that my eyes saw, with the revelations I had, and with the confirmations I got from my daily devotionals, I simply stood on the grounds of faith that Dike would be alright.

Prior to the two donor families appearing, Dr. Neelam would tell me, "Chi, Dike is not getting any better". She kept on praying for an angel to appear to save the little boy.

"Chi, look at his report, his albumin is so low," she had said to me on one of those days.

Diarrhoea was almost always constant and although he sometimes had appetite for food, his system could not digest the food.

He was taking a cocktail of medication and these were all to fortify his system. Each time we discussed his challenge, I became weepy and as I would leave Dr. Neelam's office walking back to the apartment, I would hear a voice say, "But this child is not sick and is not ill, he just has a liver condition which his body is struggling with." Dike did not know there was anything wrong with him but was only uncomfortable most times with the itching which sometimes overwhelmed him.

About a month earlier, after I had seen Dr. Neelam and as we both left her consulting room, she had stopped mid-way down the stairs to lament that God had not yet sent an angel to save our poor child. I mumbled that God does things at His own will and not on our own time. Dr. Neelam paused and said something to me which shocked me.

"Chi, I think you should at this time go back home and concentrate on taking care of your three daughters."

I was speechless for a moment and as we parted, I said to her, "Maam, God has not yet told me!"

I had not given up on God, and so was not ready to go home to a hopeless situation when my God had already told me that Dr. Neelam and her team had the rod to part the Red Sea on my child's behalf.

I did not know how it would happen but I was convinced without any iota of doubt, that it would happen and I often said to those I communicated with, including my husband that I would come home with a bouncing baby boy who had a new life. When I looked at Dike, I did not see his protruding abdomen or his skin which had gone from fair to chocolate, to light and finally to very dark brown scaly itchy skin as a result of the bile at the end stage of the disease. His looks were appalling and one could not believe the handsome Indian looking boy with curly hair at birth had transformed into this stunted little chap with green eyes and a distended abdomen. Dike looked like a creature from outer space and occasionally some Indian children while in the consulting lobby would stare at him and run back to their mamas.

It was on that day after Dr. Neelam spoke that I started seeing clearly, that each of the blood tests and the doctor's reports came back worse than the previous, yet despite the facts of the medical reports, whenever we were in our apartment, I saw the child grow stronger by the day.

As Mike and I discussed with Dr. Soin on the development with Priya Ahuja, the surgeon said we also had the option of looking out for another donor family, but since it had taken that long to get those two donor options, it could take months before any other donor option comes forth. I told him we had no choice but to wait for the six weeks treatment, considering the fact that we had spent time and money once again going through all the pre-requisite procedures before the transplant, and for the second time sat with the committee which was in itself half a day's wait, with the long list of patients and their donors awaiting clearance for various organ donations.

The feat of collecting reports and legal paper works had been done under immense pressure and we had achieved that twice within a week, including the public holidays in between with the many Indian celebrations that period. There was so much pressure on our already very tight daily schedule and I was also very convinced that the long awaited solution had been found. My spirit was at rest as Dr. Soin spoke and Mike and I agreed to wait for Priya to recover. Dr. Soin agreed with us and expressed his conviction that waiting for her recovery was the best option we had, especially with the good omen of their having showed up a few days after our scheduled surgeries with the Jhejani's were aborted. It was indeed a miracle to scale the entire medical test, therefore we knew that God had given us the desired solution and all that remained was the perfection of that promise. We parted and I was in high hopes as we waited for the long six weeks to come to pass.

Mike decided to return home to take care of things so he could plan a return trip, as the surgery was rescheduled for the 26th of June 2009, exactly six weeks from the time Priya's treatment commenced. My aunt Adeline who was scheduled to come in a few days to the surgery still came as planned and a few days later, Mike left us while we carried on.

The Charismatic Movement

I had been acquainted with the Lady Cecilia, a devout Catholic who attended mass daily at the cathedral in the heart of Delhi. Whenever we drove by the cathedral, she would make the sign of the cross from her forehead to her chest and across her bosom, signifying the Trinity (The Father, The Son and The Holy Ghost). She would often tell me that she had to come back to church later in the day for the evening mass. She always invited me but I am not Roman Catholic so had no compulsion to attend mass with her, despite the fact that I needed a place of worship for my spiritual strength and also to fellowship with fellow believers.

As we awaited surgery, Dr. Neelam said we needed donors for the blood bank. When I told her I had no one to ask to donate blood, she said she had expected I would have made friends in Delhi having lived in the city for a few months. She screamed at me in disappointment.

"Get up and do something; go find a place of worship. Don't you know that it is in such places that you can find spiritual strength?"

I was ashamed hearing those words from her.

In her usual manner, she softened her voice and urged me to

go out and make friends, and I realised I truly needed to mingle. Dr. Neelam was always right and one never really knows what could be achieved until an effort is made.

I spoke to Cecilia and she agreed to take me to see the priest at the Cathedral. We went to mass and afterwards we met with the amiable priest who advised we meet with the charismatic group of the church. They had rounded up their activities for the day but asked us to come to their next meeting; we left assuring him we would come.

We went back a few days later and were received in their prayer room. They sat on mats in a relaxed atmosphere as they worshipped. They shared testimonies, played the instruments as they sang choruses and they prayed the Rosary.

Before I got the chance to do a proper introduction and state my need, the leader of the group told them that we were from Nigeria and patients in the nearby hospital and needed blood donors. He asked if any of them would be willing to donate blood and three hands went up immediately. I was pleasantly surprised for I did not imagine that complete strangers would be so open to give so generously for a cause they had nothing to benefit from.

We were told one or two persons more might show up to give as well. All they needed was information on when and where to donate the blood, so I gave them my phone number; they then gave us audience to speak. I addressed the group telling them about Dike who was scheduled to undergo a liver transplant and needed blood donation as a mandatory contribution from a patient's family, friends and well-wishers to the blood bank. After the talk, we relaxed and worshipped with them. Before we left, I assured them that my Aunt and I would bring Dike to worship with them regularly. I recalled the words of Dr. Neelam again and had no doubt that God had used her once again to give me spiritual direction and a life lesson at a time of great need, for I needed more than blood at this low period of my life.

On Monday the 11th of May 2009, I received a call from one of the volunteers informing me that four of them would come to donate blood and we agreed to meet at the blood bank. We met the next day; I was so touched that they took out time to come as they had pledged. After the mandatory tests, one of the potential donors was not eligible to donate although I don't remember why but it was not as a result of any health challenge. Afterwards, I bought them some snacks at the hospital restaurant despite their resisting my intention to host them. We took some pictures before we parted on a happy note and once more, I glorified the Lord for His provision.

Throughout that day, I pondered on the ease of conviction these young Indians had in donating blood. I knew there was something that drove them to donate and I needed to understand this. Eventually, I would understand that it was a result of their values which was deeply rooted in their culture. They were open minded and kind, and did not have quest for personal benefit, which even made them resist my plea to treat them to lunch.

Indeed it was easy for the Indians to donate blood to the blood banks available in the hospitals. They were compelled to donate their blood to the hospital blood banks, or give their hair to the shrines as part of their birthday celebrations or an anniversary. They were aware that donating blood saves lives so whenever there was an emergency that required blood, the hospital just went to the blood bank to get some. This is only possible in a society where the citizens are well informed on the usefulness of a blood bank.

In my own part of the world, people are often sceptical about blood donations as there are so many myths associated with blood. Occultism, witchcraft and ignorance also deter people from donating. It is my belief that we need to be more educated about the benefits of blood donation and to have better orientation for the hospital administrators, the patients and the general population. This would save many lives.

In India, before a surgery is done, one is given notice by the hospital of the amount of blood needed and urged to find donors. The scenario was that if Dike and I need more than thirty pints of blood each, all we needed to do was get as many people as we could to donate blood. The blood is sent to the blood bank, so if we could raise 90 pints of blood for the blood bank, it simply made the hospital blood bank run effectively. We did not have to use up what we brought. One just needed to understand that in a worst case scenario, where we lost a lot of blood after surgery and would require much more blood than we had deposited, the blood bank will not say to us, "sorry your blood deposit has been exhausted, go and find more donors".

As the days progressed and with my Aunt around to support me, having settled in with Dike and I, we lived one day at a time in anticipation of God's solution for our challenge. Mike had since left and called us every day.

My aunt and I share the same birthday which is the 29th of May. On our birthday we chose to stay indoors to celebrate quietly. Later that day, I went to the hospital to pick up Dike's test and take to Dr. Neelam to review as usual. I informed her it was my birthday as well as my Aunt's and she wished us a happy birthday inviting us to come for a little party in her office to celebrate us the next day.

On the 30th of May 2009, we dressed up and went as invited and saw that she had actually ordered some cakes, finger foods and some drinks. She also had the members of her paediatric team join in our celebration in her very tight office. We were elated at her thoughtfulness and care, and we expressed our gratitude to her and her team. Afterwards, my aunt and I treated ourselves to a pair of sunglasses as birthday gifts. Despite Dike's condition, we chose to feel good about ourselves.

Assurance In The Storm

As we prepared to go in for surgery, I received a telephone call from one of our father figures, an elder in Port-Harcourt.

"My daughter, please come home. Leave Dike in the hands of God and do not dare God by sacrificing a part of you because the greatest plan can go wrong on the operating table," he said.

As he spoke I silently agreed with him. I knew it was needless to argue with him. There is an Igbo proverb which goes "it is 'no' that usually cause problems" loosely explained as "a negative response usually breeds resistance". I had already taken my instruction from the Lord and I had the blue print of the journey as revealed to me, so I instantly made up my mind to disregard the elder's words of wisdom and his genuine concern for us. I had to document it to add to the testimony we were about to witness as I maintained my belief that one will find his essence in life when he is willing to die for a cause he believes in.

Mike had called me the day before to tell me to expect a phone call from the elder. He had advised me not to argue when I received the phone call and I was glad for the prior notice about the call. The elder called me again 5 minutes later to further dissuade me from the surgery. I still did not argue with him for my mind was made up.

As we went through the storm, we anchored with the Charismatic Movement in worship. On Wednesday the 13th of May 2009, I went for our first meeting with Dike and my aunt Adeline. It was the day after the group members had donated blood at the hospital Blood Bank.

Most of the young members were students from different institutions of higher learning within and outside Delhi. They were bold and committed Christians who had faced stiff adversity having renounced their parent's various religious beliefs to embrace Christianity. They often went on evangelism and struggled to win souls for Christ. India with a population of 1.5 billion at that time, had a Christian population at about 1% with most living in Chennai. In totality, there were about 150 thousand Christians and I considered us privileged to be in the midst of those young, vibrant and courageous Charismatic Catholics in Delhi. Their mode of worship was very similar to Pentecostals which I am familiar with; the only difference being their praying with the rosary.

What amazed me most about them was their total commitment to the things of God. They received us with so much warmth and were enthusiastic about saying special prayers for Dike. They often prayed for long hours after the fellowship meetings in a chapel within the church premises. Some of them would even pray all day and all night at a stretch.

A member of the charismatic group, Suareph, was particularly excited to meet us especially as we are from the Igbo tribe of southern Nigeria. He and his friends had read Chinua Achebe's most popular book "*Things Fall Apart*" and asked a lot of questions which we were willing to answer. They had studied the book as a literary text in school and looked forward to seeing and understanding more about Nigeria, especially the Igbos of the eastern region of Achebe's ancestry.

They were particularly curious about the kola-nut and what it represented. My aunt and I were amused and promised to get some kola-nuts for them when someone would come from Nigeria. I knew Mike would be back in a few weeks for the surgery, so I made plans to have him bring some, which he did. They were quite satisfied and excited about this. I explained that the kola-nut is grown in the western regions of Nigeria, eaten by the northerners but most revered by the Igbos of the south. Whenever there are guests to a household, at a ceremony in the community, or at a gathering of Igbos in or out of the country, the elders break the kola-nut as a sign of peace, saying prayers or libation and blessings. It is usually a sign of peace and wellbeing and this remains one of the most revered traditions amongst the Igbos.

My aunt and I nicknamed the young Suareph "Achebe", for he looked like an intellectual. We believed he would become a professor someday.

On the 3rd of June 2009, I received a phone call from Ugo Nkwocha, a close family friend who lives in London with his family. I was so delighted to hear from him. Talking to Ugo was refreshing as we shared our burdens and gave each other renewed strength.

We had gone to the hospital earlier that day to see Dr. Neelam with Dike's test result. Dr. Neelam explained to me that Dike's protein levels were very low at 2.5g/L and his glucose level was also very low; with less sugar in his system, the jaundice could affect his brain.

She also said Dike was developing oedema as his legs were beginning to retain fluid. She recommended a strict diet for Dike. I called my aunt into the consulting room on Dr. Neelam's advice for she believed so much in a family support system, especially in a crisis period. I was truly concerned, and I felt guilty that perhaps I had not been feeding Dike properly.

Despite the strength I derived from my belief, a visit to the doctors would often leave me shaken. I realised that Dike was truly at the end stage of the liver disease and the signs were becoming more obvious; I felt bewildered as the days went by. Nevertheless, I told Dr. Neelam that it was amazing that Dike was becoming stronger despite all the negative blood reports. She told me that she now believes Dike has biliary atresia since his GGT had consistently been on the rise.

As we left Dr. Neelam's office, I remembered the devotional message during my stay at the Apollo Hospital in Chennai the previous year -"The Doctors' report vs. God's report". I chose God's report.

We went to INA market to buy the recommended food for Dike which was tofu, dal and soya-bean, as well as other things we needed.

The following day, we went to the Cathedral to ask the Catholic Father where we could buy Christian books. He directed us to St Paul's Bookshop in Connaught Place, which is in the very busy New Delhi business district. Our taxi driver, Mr. Girish, took us there; it reminded us of the very busy Tinubu Square in Lagos, Trafalgar Square in London and The Grand Central Station in New York. The Connaught Place is a tourist attraction, surrounded by government ministries and parastatals, shops, and businesses in general. We were quite delighted to find the bookshop where we purchased some Christian C.D's for Dike, a Don Moen CD a book titled *10 minutes to Creativity* by R.R. Ravi and some other exciting collections.

Our outing that day was like a breadth of fresh air; I acknowledged that sometimes miracles come in little doses as God carries us step after step through our challenges. I usually spent my days writing, reading, watching movies on television and attending to Dike. It was a tough season in my life, but I made up my mind to make the best out of it.

I always see every challenge as an adventure in life and a phase I know will come and go. As a poet and a lover of aesthetics, I know that context dramatically shapes perspectives as it always influences what we experience as content in any given situation. From this perspective, the principle also holds that the people we interact with and the places we dwell in and visit, always influences who we are and how we live.

I had spent the first half of the year in India, reading several books and watching many movies. The film that impressed me the most was "Freak the Mighty" with a storyline about strength of character, hope and perseverance. I am inspired to write poetry from my situations in life and after watching the film, I realised I had so much potential, far more than I could behold. I was able to connect the story to Dike's situation and knew that God always allows us use the challenges we face to do great exploits for His glory. I was convinced that with all the revelations I had, Dike would be a child that would be watched on the big screen someday. I also connected with Dr. Neelam and her team's exploits as we anticipated with great faith that something great was about to happen.

Handling Dreams

The text for Friday the 5th of June 2009 was titled "Handling Dreams", with the text taken from Habakkuk 2:3.

> "And the Lord answered me and said, "write the vision and make it plain upon tables, that he may run that readeth it. For the vision is yet for an appointed time, but at

the end it shall speak and not lie; though it tarry, wait for it; because it will surely come, it will not tarry."
Habakkuk 2:3

Watching "Freak the Mighty" had greatly motivated me, my dreams and revelations and above all, Dike's story clearly showed me that I had to do something with my hands, and my imagination. As I left the St. Paul's bookshop with my newest prized possession a day earlier, I was glad that I was finally beginning to consider an aspect of my life that was yet to manifest, the skill of creative writing.

Pastor Adeboye wrote that dreams can be a very strong motivating force which could see you through life's difficulties. In his words,

"Never give up on your dream...your dream will surely materialize. But always remember God has an appointed time for the dream to manifest. You shall not die before the time of manifestation. Are you poor but God has told you or shown you that you shall be rich? Hold on for it shall be fulfilled at God's appointed time. Never fight against a God given dream for your response will determine the outcome."

Visit To The Taj Mahal

One day, after our consultation with Dr. Neelam, a member of her team, Dr. Sakchi asked me how we were spending our time in Delhi. She had earlier asked me to visit the malls and see some interesting places in town. This time again she suggested we take a tour to the Taj-Mahal in Agra, which is one of the Seven Wonders of the World. I had no idea where it was located. I thought of the Taj-Mahal Hotel in Mumbai which had been the target of a terrorist attack a few months earlier. I didn't realise they were not in the same location.

So on the 5th of June 2009, we set out on a trip to Agra to see the Taj-Mahal. We left Delhi at 7am and it turned out to be a four and half hour journey. It was a fascinating outing which enabled us see and experience life in the outskirts of the city. I was struck by the density of the population, even on the outskirts of Delhi. The only open spaces I recall seeing were the farmlands. It was a welcome relief to see that India was serious about agriculture.

The Taj Mahal was awesome. The beautiful edifice reflected different colours at different times of the day as a result of the translucent limestone used in its construction. Everything about the architecture was symmetrical and perfectly calculated, such that whatever you had on the right was replicated on the left with accuracy. Only the tomb of the King, which was an afterthought from the architectural plan, appeared out of order for he had not intended that he would be buried next to his beautiful wife.

Unfortunately, our visit was in the month of July when the sun was at its peak, and the day was extremely hot and humid. The excruciating heat and irritation was unbearable for Dike and an unnecessary torture. Dike's dressing was reduced to a cotton pinafore and diapers. He had to be powdered every few minutes as his body was constantly drenched in sweat. Our tour guide advised an evening entry to Agra and an overnight stay in a hotel to enable one view the breadth taking sunset over the limestone edifice of the Taj Mahal.

An outing that should have been a day's tour was hastily done in less than one hour as we had to leave Agra. We stopped at a small bazaar and bought one silk George material as souvenir. We arrived Delhi at 8.10p.m tired but ecstatic, even Dike had enjoyed the time out.

Hello Or Save Our Souls

The Open Heavens of Sunday the 7th of June 2009 with text taken from 2 Kings 6: 5 stated that 'if you are really in need, it will show in the way you open your mouth to God.' When the axe head fell in that Bible passage, the one handling it screamed "Alas, Master! For it was borrowed". In the New Testament, blind Bartimaeus cried to the Lord in a way that could not be ignored (Mark 10:46-52). In Psalms 50:15, God says, "And call upon me in the day of trouble: I will deliver thee and thou shall glorify me."

Pastor Adeboye is of the belief that Africans see more miracles than in the developed countries because in Africa, there is no faith in the economic and social system. As such, we that believe are left with Jesus as our only hope for survival, whereas the developed countries have everything working for them especially for the sick, the less privileged and even the disabled. Therefore, they are not under pressure to call on the Lord for deliverance from trouble.

If blind Bartimaeus had not spoken, perhaps he would have remained blind forever. Ask yourself if your call is a 'Hello' or an SOS call for help.

Reading this text pacified me for I knew that It was an SOS to God as we awaited the deliverance of our son Dike. I knew that our sufficiency was of God and held on to the belief that the tide will turn around soon. My Aunty Adeline and I consistently prayed about life after Dike's challenge. How were we to move forward on our return home? I thought of going back to school to obtain a master's degree and finally a doctorate or even a law degree, which I had been nursing since my university days. But I did not think too much for I needed to finish first with the things before me and let God direct me as I already told Him my desires.

Late that night, my brother Tonye called to say he had just

arrived in China and he would visit us after our surgeries. I shared with him my anxiety about building my career on our return. I spoke on the looming recession which Mike was already experiencing in his business. I was also becoming aware of the financial obligations especially after a successful transplant and other family responsibilities including my mother-in-law's failing health. He told me not to worry but to get home first for he was missing me; this was a response which pacified me.

The Wilderness Days

The Open Heavens Message for the 9th of June 2009 was titled "Service in Captivity". The memory verse was from Psalm 137: 4 which read "How shall we sing the Lord's song in a strange land?" It was a difficult time for me at that point to write regularly and I regard it as the wilderness days. However, I still took solace in reading from the Open Heavens devotional which amazingly led me through the days and reminded me of where I was and the purpose of being there. I felt like the Israelite who God fed manna from heaven and provided a path for.

It is easy to serve God when all is well, but service during a siege or captivity makes more meaning to Him. "When you find yourself in another country, do you hide your faith in Christ?" asked Daddy G. O. I choose not to hide my faith, for God had taken me through many challenges.

On the 12th of June 2009, we went to see Dr. Neelam. It was a day to smile for Dike's test result showed he had no ascites, no oedema, and his protein and albumin levels were normal. His total bilirubin level was down to 17mg/dL. I was overjoyed; it was another miracle.

Crying is not the solution to a problem; we need to have faith to enable us partake in God's provision. The Bible in the book of Genesis tells the story of Hagar and her son Ishmael who were alone in the desert and had exhausted the water in their bottle. Hagar was scared for she knew the implications of not having water in the wilderness. Because she bitterly preoccupied her mind with negative thoughts, she could not see the well beside her. The Lord opened her eyes to see and drink from it. They eventually lived and prospered there. Looking critically, it was the baby who displayed faith through crying after which they got a desired result.

I received a similar answer when Dike cried out to me late that night.

"Mamma, mummy, mummy!"

He went on rattling for about five minutes for the first time in his life. I was stunned. Dike was talking! Feeling overwhelmed, I telephoned my aunt who had gone to sleep in her own room, to listen to our Dike calling me 'Mummy'. She was delighted to hear him speak. She came to meet me and pointed out the Open Heavens devotional message for that day, stating that it was the little boy Ishmael's cry that the Lord answered and not necessarily his mother's, relating the passage to Dike. We had another reason to remain faithful and prayerful for our desired expectations.

As we walked through our wilderness experience, my aunt and I found ways to occasionally entertain ourselves. The movie *Slumdog Millionaire* was premiering in India and as we celebrated Dike's momentary stability, we decided to join the rest of the world in watching the much celebrated film set in India. We proceeded to the theatre.

We went to Pahar Ganjh and made enquiries on how to locate a cinema to watch the movie and were directed to the Max Studio in Ghazeabad, almost an hour away. It was the nearest of the theatres where the *Slumdog Millionaire* was showing. I slumbered and woke up several times during the movie for I was totally fatigued from my daily routine and the long journey meandering through Delhi traffic. It was indeed a wonderful movie and we were glad we took out time to go see it and have a little fun as we prayerfully waited for our surgery day.

Insured Against Problems?

On our next appointment day, Dr. Neelam examined Dike's x-ray and said his heart was enlarged. She referred us to see the cardiologist the next day. With a heavy heart, we went home to pray for there was nothing else to do. We felt better afterwards and tried not to worry.

The topic of the day was titled "Insured Against Problems?" and the memory verse was taken from Psalm 72:12.

> "For He shall deliver the needy when he crieth; the poor also and him that hath no helper".
> Psalm 72:12

The message holds that while working in total obedience to God, you can still run into problems, just like in the story of the axe head that sank and was later made to float by the prophet of God. Unfortunately, those who doubt when they face such challenges, fail to understand that satan will always try to challenge any situation God has His hands upon. Satan does not threaten what he is in control of but mainly those of heavenly value. The more important a project is to God, the more challenging it would become, for satan will attack it with every weapon at his disposal.

Most people miss their destinies because when faced with a

challenge they asked "Why me?" Others claim "It's not my portion", or say "God forbid", while some others just choose the path of denial and hope that the challenge will pass just as it came. They end up losing the lesson and not benefiting from their challenge.

We knew we had a challenge with Dike's health; we also knew all we could do was hold on to God and believe He will enable us overcome.

The message for Tuesday the 16th of June 2009 was titled "Link to a Miracle" and was based on the story of the Israeli slave girl in the household of General Naaman. She suffered the pain of being separated from her family. When she found out about her master's journey to find healing for his leprous skin, she realised her time to make a difference in his situation had come. She wondered why her master had spent a fortune seeking healing when there was a prophet of God in Israel who could heal him. She realised that her presence in the General's home was to be a link to his miracle. With this understanding, she did not hesitate in telling her mistress the way to the miracle.

I realised that the wilderness experience we were having was perhaps the link to someone's blessing. I took my eyes off the negative aspects of our predicament, and allowed the Lord to use our situation to reveal and discover God's purpose for my life, and the path to fulfilling it. We can all ask God to reveal those we are meant to link to their blessings. Although the present situation may be unpleasant, we are urged to be expectant of a pleasant tomorrow.

We went to the hospital and met with Dr. Anil Sachele; he asked us to get an Echo report from the X-ray Department. On our way, we ran into Dr. Neelam. I briefed her on the morning appointment and she said Dike already had an Echo report done earlier in February therefore would not need to do another. We left and went to do the blood sampling for CMV and afterwards went back to see her.

She gave us a note to see the cardiologist, Dr. Mohanty. He was on leave, so we saw Dr. Aman Makhija instead, in his office on the 5th floor of the Sir Ganga Ram Hospital. He directed that we wait in the Echo room on the ground floor because he wanted to do the Echo himself. The results showed that Dike's heart was not enlarged but remained as it was earlier. What a relief. We praised God for what I considered another miracle and I was glad that I did not worry, for I felt there was no need to worry about things we had no control over. Moreover, having gone this far, I felt the Lord would not leave us desperate and devoid of one more miracle.

We left the hospital and went to the Max Mall in Ghaziabad to shop for Dike and his sisters; thinking we might not have a chance to shop for them after the transplant, so I felt it was best to go at that time.

Revelations

As I pondered on what to do after our surgeries, given that I might not be able to run around like I used to in the course of my business and knowing that a regular job would be unthinkable with the challenge at hand, I decided to try a new line of business. It was a prodding I knew and understood therefore I asked Cecilia, the woman who had earlier taken me to the hotel in Pahar Ganjh, to escort me to where I could buy the types of fabric Nigerian women love to wear. We went to Chandi Chawk and I selected two samples.

I believed that having stayed in India for quite a while, the Lord would give me a solution on how to sustain my family in the coming years. I needed a little more than the anticipated success of the liver transplant to justify our sojourn in India. I had thought about this while walking the streets in the various sectors of Delhi when we went to the market, church, shopping malls and even house hunting. I craved for something tangible that I would call an economic take away to justify my exposure in India.

I showed my aunt the fabric I got from Chandi Chawk and we deliberated on the experience of the day and then analysed the potential business of fabrics back home. By the next day, I had a clear answer to my quest. I was to go back to the market, make a deposit on selected fabrics and after the surgery, return to pay up and collect the items.

I was so sure the answer I got came from above and I was excited yet peaceful. I did as I was led and for the next four years, the fabric business sustained us. I was grateful to God that I heeded when I did, for it provided for us all through the challenges of the first four post-transplant years.

The next day, we went for our appointment with Dr. Neelam and she confirmed that Dike's chest was clear and strong enough for his transplant. We hoped that Mrs. Ahuja was getting stronger from her ailment and would be totally fit to undergo the surgery by the proposed date of the 26th of June 2009.

Dr. Neelam told us she would take a five-day vacation with her family and would be back right in time for our surgeries. She said her life was wrapped around the lives of her patients therefore she could only take very short vacations. She would never leave her transplanted patients and go on vacation, so it was best she went immediately and then be back right before our surgeries.

On the night of the 23rd of June 2009, I had a revelation. In my dream I had another confirmation that we were treading the right path. I saw myself walking tall and courageous in the face of adversity. When I travel long distance, I usually find comfort in the air rather than on the road since I have no phobia for high places. I actually feel that when I am in an aircraft, I am a soul closer to my Lord.

In the dream, I found myself on a very high telecommunications mast with a formation like a bridge constructed with vertical bars. The angular formation was in the form of a right angled triangle where one point was higher than the one preceding it. I was with my university roommate, Stella Amechi. I found myself gliding on the top rod that connected the vertical bars and occasionally I held the bars and jumped from one to another the way a monkey jumps from tree to tree in the jungle. Each time I got to the apex of the mast, I would display some acrobatic feats and then glide down again to the base while my children and other spectators watched and cheered.

At some point when I got back to the apex of the mast, the pole suddenly shifted and I was left suspended and could not get to the connecting bar to glide down. I saw that my friend Stella was panicking at the other lower extreme. As I remained suspended, I thought about the safest way to get down. After a while, the station manager came forward and took hold of the main pole of the mast that had me suspended. He swiftly pushed it away as if it were on rollers and then bent it sideways in the opposite direction with ease while I firmly held on to the bar, adjusting my position as the bar bent downwards. The spectators, sensing what the station manager was trying to achieve, ran forward to assist in bending the bar horizontally. As the pole came lower, I jumped down like a paratrooper, running till I came to a gradual stop.

Stella immediately confronted the station manager, accusing him of being mean to me even though his actions worked in my favour. His intention was to sabotage my acrobatic feat, which unfortunately for him, eventually terminated at the same point it was supposed to. His bending the pole had kept us all in suspense, but ended up in a positive boomerang effect. In other words, moving the pole far from its original location and bending it horizontally actually catapulted me to my destination even faster than I would have gotten there through the acrobatic feats.

The spectators did not understand the challenge we had faced. I told the station manager that one of the lessons I had learnt in life and from that particular experience was that in the face of adversity, I always find succour by being open minded. It ensured I remained flexible both in body and in spirit which usually gets me a desired reward. I realised that all the delays did not matter but were all in the perfect will of God for us.

I woke up and realised that I had once more received another revelation that the challenge we faced would yield a positive result.

Mike returned to Delhi in time for our surgeries.

"D" Day - 25th June 2009

The six-week wait finally came to an end and all was set for pre-surgery admissions. We all went into hospital on the 24th of June 2009 to be monitored for the next 48 hours. We had a hectic day once more, running the final work-up tests; my spirit was high. Very early in the morning, I was woken up with the news that the medical team had made an impromptu decision to move us into the theatre and start the surgeries.

Dike and Priya would first be wheeled into two separate theatres and after about an hour or two, Haresh and I would be wheeled in to two other separate theatres. The team decided that since four of us were in good health, it was best to begin the surgeries rather than wait for another 24 hours. We already knew that if any of us had a cough, cold, diarrhea, fever or any form of stress, the surgeries would be postponed once more. It was also best to carry out the four surgeries concurrently, so for the next thirty-six hours, the team of thirty-six medical personnel performed the swap liver transplant, which was recorded as a medical breakthrough in the field of liver transplantation.

Although I went in feeling very elated that at last Dike had come to the end stage of the liver cirrhosis and would emerge a new child, it would not be devoid of blood, pain and some huge scars. I recall I felt a lot of pressure and deep pain while the surgery went on despite the anaesthesia. I continued to moan while in the subconscious, and at some point when I fidgeted I heard the surgeon ask for more anaesthesia to be administered. When I came to, I found myself in the intensive care unit.

I recall that when I awoke, I felt Mike's presence in the room and the euphoric feeling that I had come out of deep slumber. The medical attendees were watching and monitoring like hawks for 24 hours. As they talked to me, I suddenly heard someone shout that I was losing a lot of blood and in the twinkle of an eye, I slipped back into oblivion.

It would be weeks later, after I had left the hospital and when I went through my folder, that I saw the documented evidence stating I had lost a lot of blood and had to be immediately transfused with several pints of blood. Only then did I realise how easy it is for people to pass on after successful surgeries, especially in my part of the world where round the clock monitoring and total attention to detail are taken for granted. At that same moment my cousin Chizoba Onuoha in Lagos had a revelation about me and immediately raised an altar on our behalf. I got to know the details a few years later.

I was in the ICU for three days before I was finally moved to the private room for one more week, making a total of 12 day stay in hospital. Mike had come back to India a week to the surgeries to be my attendant, while my Aunt nursed Dike. It was a slow and steady recovery and the Lord was with us all. I went to see Dike a few times in his semi-conscious state in the ICU and he was later moved to the private ward.

The Ahujas had their own challenge. While Haresh made full and quick recovery like I did, his wife spent a longer time in the ICU. When she finally left the hospital, she was frail and could no longer walk. She had to undergo a series of physiotherapy sessions to enable her walk again. Organ donors usually have fewer challenges, unlike the recipients who face the possibility of rejection and other issues due to their state of health prior to the transplant necessitating a longer stay in the intensive care units.

Being in the intensive care unit involves a two-hourly blood sampling to determine if there are signs of infections which could trigger a rejection of the transplanted organ.

Dike, having been stabilized, was moved out of the ICU on Saturday the 4th of July 2009. Mike and I, in company of the medical attendees, wheeled him to the private room and I was cautioned not to stay long with him as I was also recuperating.

When I got back to the apartment, I saw a book sticking out of the landlord's belongings in the basement room where my aunt occupied. Our landlord, Chibs Aman had his family belongings neatly tucked away in the basement while they lived elsewhere within the neighbourhood. It was a collection of classic stories for children and I was thrilled to read it.

There was the story of Corduroy, a very unattractive teddy bear with a missing button on his shirt. No child wanted him in the toy shop until one little sympathetic girl found him and wanted none other. I recalled Dike at the end stage, as he looked like an unattractive alien with green eyes, a protruding abdomen and dark, scaly and itchy skin. Corduroy's story was an instant parallel.

All the stories captivated me, and I found myself once more fantasizing on writing similar children's stories in addition to the story on Dike's phenomenal life. I could write such simple stories and could also write down my dreams and revelations as compilations of stories. The fact that my mind was drifting towards this revelation in harmony with my skills and talents excited me. I had also recorded many songs on my phone as the revelations came to me in my sleep. Unfortunately, I lost all those recordings shortly after we returned to Nigeria. I have continued to record songs and hope to present them someday as I remain grateful to God for my talents.

I went to the hospital every two or three days to dress my scar and would stop by to see Dike. My aunt and Mike took shifts to nurse him. On Saturday, the 11th of July 2009, when I went in to see him, he was sitting on my aunt's lap with the intra-venous drip attached to his wrist. He looked so lonely and pathetic, like Corduroy the teddy bear and I felt totally helpless. Seeing us did not seem to excite him and his very sad expression broke my heart.

He had been in pain all the while as he was pricked about nine times daily for blood samples. Most times the blood did not always flow at the first prick due to his small veins; this meant that he was pricked much more than nine times. Once again, I was glad that Dr. Sakchi had informed me weeks before the surgery of what Dike would pass through with the needles, so I was emotionally prepared. I truly appreciated all the extra effort Dr. Neelam and her team made in cushioning my anxiety in our quest to save our little boy.

The Awakening

Dike often looked at his hands and wrists and probably wondered why they hurt so much. However, on this remarkable Saturday, the 18th of July 2009, I walked into the room and Dike looked at me and smiled; my heart was filled with joy. I praised the Lord and I knew that everything would be all right. I tried to make him laugh which he did in great excitement. For the first time in history, we saw Dike with his eyes cleared from jaundice and in a hilarious mood.

I took several pictures of him with my mobile phone and then gave him the phone to play his favourite music. My aunt also gave him her phone and he immediately found his favourite cricket game and started to play it. I stayed for another hour and a half then left to rest as the doctors had advised that I should not stress myself. I met Mike on my way out of the hospital and I excitedly told him of Dike's progress and he was glad. Much later, my aunt came back to the apartment and told me that Dike was still in high spirits and had crawled all over the bed. He showed his excitement when he saw his dad; we were all very excited to have a new Dike. Our excitement was greater than that of one who had just been delivered of a much awaited baby boy.

I slept at 10.00pm and woke at 11.45pm to call Mike. He said that Dike was still awake and excited, and was crawling all over the bed. His bed was the regular adult hospital bed with no breakers to stop a fall, so we worried that he could roll off the bed in his excitement. This became an extra cause to keep round the clock watch on him. He wanted to crawl on the floor most of the time but he had to be restrained.

In my euphoria, I called Sylvia to share in our joy and I also sent text messages to some of our relations back home. I sent a message to Dr. Ekeoku who was very excited. He said it was the best news he had received in years. He praised God and commended my faith. He also reaffirmed his earlier advice that I should never ever give up on our challenge.

We were very excited about Dike's recovery because just two days earlier, Mike had come back to the apartment feeling sad because Dike's hands were in pain and it made him very sober. I had observed that the IV drip on his right hand had been stopped and reset on the left hand causing him much pain. From the regular blood testing at the ICU, it was obvious he had been pricked more than a hundred times so he had every cause to be gloomy. His eyes remained focused on the wrist that hurt most and I believed he knew why it hurt so much.

Mike told me Dike was missing me, however I could not go to him as often as I would have loved to. I was also in deep pain and was carrying a drain bag attached to my abdomen. The doctors had emphasized to Mike and my aunt that I keep away from attending to Dike as much as possible, therefore I only saw him briefly every other day when I went to the hospital to dress my wound.

A day earlier, I had jokingly told Mike not to worry about Dike being so quiet for his son is just like him, but when he smiles he is like me. Little did we know that in less than twenty four hours, Dike's countenance would totally change to that of laughter, and that of course pacified our souls. My aunt later told me that after I left the hospital, the doctors and nurses came on ward rounds and were excited to see Dike in such a jovial mood. The challenge remained in watching him closely as he constantly tried to jump off the bed and crawl all over the floor.

As I gradually recuperated, I observed that the drain pouch I carried did not drain for three days, from the 13th to the 16th of July. While I rested, I minimized the use of the spirometer I was given after the surgery for my lung exercise. However, at 7.30 pm on that Saturday the 16th, I suddenly had a very foul smelling discharge that measured 65mls. On Sunday morning at 11.15am, I had more of the smelly discharge so went for dressing at the hospital. As I was being dressed, some more very smelly discharge was drained so I went to see the surgeon and he prescribed Amikay injections with a twice daily dose. On Monday morning after I took the dose, I felt feverish so on Tuesday I went to see Dr. Soin after he called to know how I was doing. He prescribed some more medication which I took and got better.

A few days later while waiting to see Dr. Soin for a follow up, I heard the great news about Bella and Hawii's successful surgeries. Dr. Soin saw me waiting and asked that I go to the casualty department so the doctors on duty could attend to me. I got there and waited for several hours without being attend to. I went back to report to Dr. Soin and while waiting to see him, I met a Nigerian man and his son. They were excited to see a fellow Nigerian. The father introduced himself as Alhaji Usman and his son as Ahmed. They came from Kwara State with his wife Alhaja Salimatu who had struggled with liver disease for nine years. They had spent a lot consulting various hospitals yet none gave her the right diagnosis or suggested that she seek medical advice outside Nigeria.

It was only after she met another lady from her state, who had also had a liver transplant at the Sir Ganga Ram Hospital, that she understood that the solution to her ailment was a liver transplant. Alhaja and her family have visited us a few times and we have remained in synergy to source medications from India following almost a decade of survival. Despite our religious differences, our relationship has been great and one born out of a mutual quest for life and encouragement in the face of adversity. This remains one of the life lessons I learnt in our quest for a medical solution.

On the 22nd of July 2009, I developed a high fever again and by 4.00pm I had 20mls of a very smelly discharge seep into my drain bag. I was glad I was still carrying the drain bag for the discharge could have poisoned my system. In the evening a day earlier, I had seen Dr. Mehta Naimish who had spoken to the radiologist about the injection and medication I was placed on. I was advised to complete the course of injections and afterwards have a scan and blood sampling to enable them take a decision on what to do next.

On the 23rd of July, my Aunt, Dike and I went for an appointment with Dr. Soin. He reviewed Dike's medication by reducing his Tacrolimus daily dose and added OCID. He said he would inform Dr. Neelam of the review. He also informed us that Priya Ahuja had started walking and was gradually getting better. He said he would give her another fifteen days, before calling the media conference to celebrate our success story. He turned to Dike and said, "I'm going to splash you all over the news".

We left Dr. Soin's office very elated that Priya was getting stronger and had started walking, though with some assistance. Celebration time would soon be due in honor to our Lord for delivering us all from the challenges we had been through.

Meanwhile, on the 22nd of July 2009, Mike had gone to the Immigration Office to get our clearance. Having gotten extensions for us twice, he was informed that we had exhausted the maximum clearance in Delhi. He was asked to go to Chennai to extend our visas and transfer our files to New Delhi, since we had entered India through Chennai. For this purpose, Mike had to get a letter from Dr. Neelam stating why we could not physically travel for our clearance. He flew out that night of the 23rd and got into Chennai at midnight.

By Thursday, my body drained another 15ml. We walked to hospital to meet with Dr. Soin and by the time we got back home, I had a 50ml collection of very smelly fluid but the fever had abated.

On the 30th of July 2009 we saw Dr. Neelam and she briefed us on the proposed media conference. She said since our swap liver transplant was the first in medical history, it would be a major celebration for the Ezeanya and the Ahuja families, and a great plus for the medical team at Sir Ganga Ram Hospital. We talked about Dike and I reminded her that his name means "The Mighty Warrior in Battle".

She apologized for not giving us a date to enable us plan ahead, especially as Mike was already booked to leave that night to attend to our children, his ailing mother and also his business.

Bella And Hawii

On the 21st of July 2009, my friend Bella a single parent Kenyan had her surgery with her 8 month old son Hawii. He also suffered from biliary atresia like Dike and had done an unsuccessful Kasai earlier in another hospital. We had met them in the course of consultations with the doctors and would eventually become good friends. As long as we were all from Africa, the doctors called us sisters. Bella and Hawii's surgeries were successful but filled with challenges. To the glory of God, they both pulled through, especially her son, who had been delivered from the clutches of death several times.

At midnight on the 29th July 2009, Dr. Neelam sent me an SMS to enquire of our wellbeing. She asked us to pray for Hawii who had undergone a stormy course of four surgeries in one week. I had seen Bella earlier in the day and she narrated her ordeal to me. Dr. Neelam confirmed that after Hawii's transplant, he developed a blood clot and had to be operated on. As he was recovering, he had a ruptured intestine, and then was diagnosed with a heart problem. For these reasons Dr. Neelam could not sleep and had to ask us to pray for the child.

She said she sees me as a prayerful person and also sees my aunty as a prayer warrior. We were happy that the doctors at least, acknowledged that the God we serve was able to bring about changes in our challenging situations. We have never ceased praying for them.

He Stood And Walked

On Saturday the 1st of August 2009 at about 2am, my Aunt carried Dike and I was compelled to ask her to put him down to walk. She did and Dike stood up without support. He took the first step and a second step and a third and in excitement he just kept on walking. We were amazed that in just one day he stood without support and then just walked. We were excited and had yet another reason to praise the Lord. Dike was 1 year and 7 months when he stood and walked!

The next day, Sunday the 2nd of August, my friend Ebere Mbaegbu came in from Abuja to stay with us. She had volunteered to come stay with us so we planned that she would arrive just before my aunt departs. Aunty had planned to stay for one month but had ended up spending a little over three months with us. We were very grateful because her stay also enabled Mike go home to take care of other issues.

At noon on Monday the 3rd of August 2009, we all went for a briefing for the media conference in Dr. Neelam's office. Afterwards, we went to the garden to meet with the medical team who welcomed us and the Ahujas. We had a photo session in the hospital auditorium which they said was the preamble to the media conference. We exchanged pleasantries with the medical team and hospital authorities.

One of the very impressive personalities we met that day was the charming elderly Dr. B.K. Rao. We later learned that he was the Chairman of the Sir Ganga Ram Hospital. We eventually dispersed in great excitement knowing that our mission in India had been one of great accomplishment.

On the 14th of August 2009, Sylvia called to discuss life in Nigeria with Dike after the transplant. She was concerned about how we would cope with the check-ups, tests and sourcing of medication. Being a medical doctor, she knew the post-transplant challenges could be overwhelming. My childhood friend Chinelo Omesuh-Ofoche also called from the USA to also discuss this new phase of our lives. She suggested we relocate to any of the developed countries as a sacrifice for Dike's sake. Ebere, who was with me also suggested we fill out the U.S. Diversity Visa forms or seek Canadian immigration. I knew these suggestions came because they all felt concern for us, and I acknowledged they made sense but I needed to hear from God before taking a decision.

The message in the Open Heavens devotional for 17th of August 2009 was titled "The Alternative is Better" with the text taken from Haggai 2:3-9. The message from Haggai gave me the encouraging words I needed.

> "The glory of this latter house shall be greater than the former saith the Lord of Hosts and this place will I give peace saith the Lord of Hosts."
> Haggai 2:9

The prophecy here is whatever you are today should be accompanied by an attitude of gratitude as the best is yet to come. As long as you remain in the Lord, your tomorrow will be better than your today; for the Lord in His nature often preserves the best for last. This was confirmed at the wedding in Cana of Galilee, where the best wine was brought in last. Also concerning covenants, the New Testament was released as a better version of the Old Testament.

Having read this message, I held unto Dike and proclaimed blessings upon him acknowledging that indeed, he is a destined child, on an assignment. I prayed that God will never replace him but rather empower him to fulfil his purpose on earth wherever he chooses as our dwelling place.

Standing Tall

The Open Heavens Devotional message for the 19th of August 2009 was titled "Why River Jordan?" with text taken from 2Kings 2: 13–14. The message here held that Elisha was instructed by God to use Elijah's mantle to strike the water. The river Jordan parted in two and Elisha was able to cross to the other side. We are told that whenever the Lord asks us to do something in a particular way, just do it even if you do not understand why - as long as you understand that the instruction is from God. This is because the Lord's choice may not always be popular, but you won't get something better.

At mid-day on the 19th of August 2009, we gathered once more in the hospital auditorium, the same location of our photo shoot. My aunt had already left for Nigeria. The media conference which had been fixed for the 6th of August had been postponed to the 19th of August to enable Mrs. Ahuja's attendance due to her slow recovery. Eby, Dike and I first met with Dr. Neelam for a briefing and afterwards she went into the auditorium to join her team for the media conference.

An hour later, the Ahujas arrived and we were excited to see them. We took pictures with them while we waited to join the conference. After another hour, the curtains were drawn, we sprang to our feet and proceeded towards the auditorium from the right wing of the stage. Dike and I clutched hands as we took little steps forward.

To my utmost amazement, I looked on as over 60 camera men and women like a flash, stooped to capture the image of the little boy who had started walking barely three weeks back. It seemed like the press men and women bowed in obeisance to a little monarch as he beamed a smile. The cameras clicked on for almost ten minutes while the rest of us watched in awe as history was being recorded. The cameras went on as each photojournalist wanted the best pose for the evening's breaking news and the next day's headline.

As this phenomenal session unfolded before our very eyes, I stood with the Ahujas; Dike firmly holding on to my hand. He exuded self-confidence at nineteen months and it seemed like he knew that history was being made. He took the first step towards the stage in his bold stripped multi coloured shirt and adorned afro hair style. He looked very robust and his fair skin glowed as he beamed a smile at several intervals, walking with style and a little swagger.

Eventually, Dr. Soin faced the media and said,

"Ok guys, let's get on with the rest of the media presentation."

Priya Ahuja had stood for long and did not need to be subjected to much strain, so we all moved a few more steps to the auditorium. Dr. Neelam picked Dike up and placed him on the table and once more the photographers started clicking away with the rest of us behind the table. After another five minutes, Dr. Soin said "Enough guys let's move into the next phase".

It was our moment of grace and Dike indeed looked so graceful. It was the best he had ever looked in his 19 months of life and we were all excited and grateful to God. At some point he stuck out his tongue in a pose that seemed to say "I know who you guys are and I know what's up, so here I am posing for you".

After we settled in for the talks, the doctors were interviewed first then I was next and finally Haresh and Priya Ahuja were also interviewed.

I remember telling the media that it was against all odds we had ended up with our successful liver transplant testimonies. When asked questions on the challenges I had to endure, my response was simply "Your attitude determines your altitude".

Dr. Soin said that "the biggest challenge in a paired donor transplant was that all surgeries had to be done at the same time in four separate theatres. This was to ensure that the first recipient's family does not change his mind to donate to the other family's recipient when his own relative has been successfully saved, or perhaps passes on as the surgery progressed."

Dr. Rao the Chairman of the Sir Ganga Ram Hospital in his speech said,

"The swap liver transplant is a welcome innovation which will help in times of donor shortages and will encourage those who otherwise would not have gotten a matching donor, therefore will enable more lives to be saved."

Dr Neelam Mohan said that "it proved very tough to keep Dike alive, especially within the last six weeks while waiting for Priya to recover from her treatment of tuberculosis."

The Ahujas said that "knowing how difficult it was to find a donor, they had worried that their donor family might not wait for Priya to recover and be paired with them."

I knew when we met with the Ahujas, the Lord had finally provided the long awaited solution to Dike's challenge. I understood that having waited so long for the right donor to come our way, there was no need to look any further; we believed that the Lord had answered the prayer. I had inner peace, unlike the impression with the Jhejanis whom we had met earlier on. I recalled that I had told Dr. Soin that we would have no choice but to wait the six weeks for Priya to recover. If the Lord had kept Dike that long with our daily testimonies, then He would keep him for another six weeks to make our testimonies complete.

I was sure that the Lord would finish the work, to prove that He is God and to establish His words through the revelations and frequent miracles He had ordered me to document.

After Dr. Neelam gave the closing speech, we were asked a lot of questions; different media houses wanted an exclusive live presentation of all of us. Lunch was served in the lobby of the conference hall after the two-hour session with the media. The media continued to engage with us until there was little food left to eat. They all gradually left after they had had their fill of food and information.

Dr. Neelam told me that I had taught her a lot in life especially in my faith and trust in God. She was amazed at my recovery and was convinced that because I was so happy giving a part of my liver my positive energy enabled me get back quickly on my feet. She told me that she was delighted for she never heard me complain of pain but saw me smiling and full of love whenever we met. She also told me that Dike was one of the most amazing patients she ever treated. His story was phenomenal and so was his recovery. Dr Neelam, Eby, Dike and I were the last to leave the auditorium.

We went back to the apartment to unwind and relax after the hectic day, only to be called shortly afterwards to get ready to be picked up at 6pm for an 8pm live session with Sahara TV, which comprises of a group of media houses. There was no time for us to unwind as we had hoped; we hurriedly ate, dressed up and left. We meandered through very heavy traffic for the next hour for what should have been a twenty minute drive on a traffic free day. The driver had doubted if we would meet up with the live broadcast, but with his expertise on the routes, he was able to get us to the station at 8.10pm.

The program was already airing with Dr. Neelam and Dr. Sanjiv Segal, who was the attending doctor to the Ahujas. When they took a break, we were beckoned to quietly come in and join the next session. Dr. Soin also arrived as we were taking our seats. Dr. Soin, Preeya, and I were interviewed with Dike on my lap while Dr. Neelam and Dr. Segal waited in the adjoining room. Haresh on the other hand was taken to another room for an exclusive interview.

We were all being interviewed in the different units but all was being aired simultaneously. Afterwards, we all regrouped and shared some pleasantries before finally dispersing for the night. It had really been a hectic but very fulfilling day.

I spoke to Mike severally times, to Tonye, Agunze, Professor Egbuonu, Aunty May, Mike's nephew Uzo, and Aunty Ida. I reminded Tonye of Pastor E.A. Adeboye's prophecy when we took Dike to him. He had said to us that "The Lord would be the one to provide the liver and we would come back to testify in the Redeemed Camp and that Dike would live to serve the Lord".

Everyone was excited for us, the joy was overwhelming. My aunt May said that the Lord had indeed taken us from infirmity to celebrity in an instant and she hopes my book on Dike would follow suit. Aunty Ida on the other hand said that with this testimony, Dike would have scholarships for life and will have free milk too and the sky would not even be his limit. Agunze said he was extremely excited about the incredible news and could not stop praising God for enabling us make history which Nigeria was yet to hear of. Professor Egbuonu said the procedure was glorious and perhaps the first of its kind. I told her the surgeon said that it was indeed a medical breakthrough; her response was "Thanks be to God".

It was interesting watching the live shows as breaking news all over the Indian media stations and beyond when we got home that night.

We slept very late and just as we woke up at 10am, we received a call from Dr. Soin's office to come over for another media interview at 11.30am. We quickly got ready and went to the hospital to find that it was another television house which did not make it to the media conference the day before. After the session with the media, we went to the transplant ward to visit Alhaja Usman who had undergone her liver transplant ten days earlier. Her son, Ahmed donated part of his liver to her and when she saw Dike and I, she broke down and wept in praise to Allah.

Back home, my uncle, Agunze and the Okogwu family had planned their children Chaka Maureen's traditional and white weddings for the 21st and 22nd of August respectively and our families, friends and well-wishers all headed for Kaduna, including my aunt Addy. Having sacrificed three months staying with us, it was time for her to go home to celebrate with our family and friends. We were grateful for all her sacrifice and prayed that the Lord would reward her for her benevolence towards us. Mike, who was also back home, took our daughters from Abuja to attend the wedding and they all had a great time.

And the telephone calls kept coming. Ken, Nathalie and their son Joshua called from Chennai, they were euphoric and had called to share in our joy. I also received a call from Sister Chika, Mike's elder sister who lives in Los Angeles. As the days progressed, I received more calls from relations at home and abroad which included my Aunt Stella, Pat Ozigbo, my neighbor in Port-Harcourt, Cousin Ucheora Onwuamaegbu from Washington D.C., Henry Ezenwa and a number of other well-wishers.

Consistently on the prayer line were the Pastors of the Everlasting Covenant Parish, Pastor Ogan and his wife Sister Evelyn, Pastor Faith, Pastor Eke Aki, his wife Ada and Brother Lekan who had initiated a fasting session for three days on our first day at the Parish. The calls just kept on coming in as everyone was ecstatic and filled with praises for the Lord's blessings.

My friend Pat called to tell me that her husband who was at work in Algeria, had called to tell her that the back page of the Guardian newspaper had our story. Irene Okoronkwo, a member of the congregation in my Abuja Parish called, and also Mike's cousin Zuby in Seattle. He was so excited for us. Chi-Chi my bosom friend also called to say she had also read the article.

Ken and his family in Chennai called again to congratulate us and said they would buy copies of all the papers we appeared in and send to us. We spared them the trouble by going out ourselves to buy them all.

We continued to see Dr. Neelam twice weekly as she monitored Dike's progress. I also went for my dressing which healed slowly. Although the hospital was nearby, it was a bit stressful having to walk there. The option of going there on a rickshaw, which is the bicycle with an umbrella chair, a common mode of transportation for short distances, was a bumpy ride and was very uncomfortable and hurt my tender abdomen. As the days progressed, it became somewhat challenging going to the hospital for the dressing because of the commute and the waiting time due to the large number of patients that required dressing from various surgeries and injuries.

As a result of these challenges, I resorted to having the local nurses dress my surgical site in the apartment. I did this only thrice and went back to the regular hospital dressing because the home service was more expensive and very painful. On enquiring why I felt more pain when dressed at home, I was told that the pain free solution used for cleaning the wound was only available in the hospitals and its use was strictly prohibited outside the hospitals. I had to go back to using the three wheeler or the rickshaw as transport to the hospital, enduring the pain of the bumpy ride.

On one of those post-surgery days, I got a pleasant call from my distant cousin Ebele Onwuamaegbu with whom I had flown to Dubai our way to India in January. She said she had sent me some money about three weeks earlier but forgot to inform me. Her gesture was a pleasant surprise and it overwhelmed me. I was grateful for her very thoughtful and kind gestures, which she repeated six years later on my visit to her home in Brooklyn with my children.

As the days progressed, Nathalie called again from Chennai to tell me that our story was in the Indian Times Magazine for the month of September. The Doctors remained pleased and excited with Dike's progress and Dr. Neelam affirmed that Dike was one of their most challenging cases yet his recovery was totally smooth and one of the fastest they had seen. It seemed more than a miracle.

My cousin Constance Ikokwu called to congratulate us. She was then a journalist with ThisDay Newspapers working as the bureau chief in the Washington D.C. office. She asked if we would authorize

ThisDay to publish our success story, to which I responded in the affirmative. She said I would receive a questionnaire via email which I would have to respond to before our story could be published. I had to find a cyber café to download the questionnaire and scan back to the office; they eventually published our story with our pictures.

Chika Peterside called me from London where she was on vacation with her family. Uncle Francis Bruce also called and I briefed him on the media coverage and he was very excited about our success story. I would later speak to my friend Ine, who had relocated from Port-Harcourt to the UK with her three daughters. As we talked on the miracle of Dike's life; she shared with me the story of the miraculous delivery of her second daughter from an undetected growth in her throat. We thanked God for delivering our children and giving them a second lease on life.

Taking On The Storm

On the 2nd of September 2009, I watched Pastor Matthew Ashimolowo of the Kingsway International Church (KICC) preach on television. He talked about the storms of life which are not always predictable. "The greater the storm," he said, "the greater the blessings". The storms could also come unpredictably; if a storm caught Jesus unpredictably then, why not us? (Matthew 8:23-27)

When a storm comes our way, we are to hold on to the Word of God and not allow fear to have a grip on us. We should not allow our brain go on a holiday and think we have gone beyond recovery. Someone else could be going through the same situation and act as if nothing was going on. He advised we do not justify the reasons for the storms of our lives, for a crisis will help us step over to the next level.

We should not let the storm get inside us but affirm that we know whom we believe. He emphasized that it is not the storm that sinks the ship but the storm water that gets into the ship that sinks it. The storm will not destroy you; it will hit a righteous man seven times and he will rise up seven times. It will push you home but not off course. You can use the negative intentions of the enemy to your advantage and get a positive result. It will not be over until you win."

As I listened to his message, I realised that Dike's battle seemed to be the easiest storm I had weathered despite its ferocity; because I had handed it over to God Almighty when I caught the revelation from the onset. I recall the Lord had said in Matthew 11:30, "For my yoke is easy and my burden is light". My positive attitude to the storm became my bedrock and the Lord granted me peace throughout the storm we faced.

I called home and got an update on the children. I remained rested and assured that all was well with them. Ugonna was in the Nigerian Turkish International College then and was blooming, gradually becoming a teenager.

On Friday the 11th of September 2009, ThisDay Newspaper in Nigeria ran our story.

Later that day, I received a call from Vivian Ezenwa and shortly afterwards from Henry Ezenwa. Their calls made my day. I also received calls from Zubeina Tanko and Chinonye Sojirin who was very weepy when we spoke.

Ebere's husband, Ugochukwu came to India and we were excited knowing our departure was fast approaching. On Saturday, Aunty Stella called from Florida and through her I spoke to my cousins in Florida. I was elated by the outpouring of love and their prayers which lightened my burden. Later in the day, Ubani Nkaginieme visited us. He had also just arrived India to visit his family after their surgery.

As the weeks progressed, we planned our departure from India. We confirmed our departure for the 28th of September 2009. We had gotten very tired of the hospital environment and the Rajinder Nager neighbourhood. We longed for home. We did what we hoped to be the last of the blood tests before our departure only for the result to come out CMV positive. I panicked when I collected the result and ran to Dr. Neelam's office, feeling very weepy and full of anxiety. In my ignorance I thought the CMV Nasba test was a test for hepatitis C. Dr. Neelam said if Dike had hepatitis C then she would have a cause to worry and I would then have a real cause to be sad for he would be dead within a year.

However, she assured me that there was no need to worry as it was just a virus which usually manifests in transplanted patients and was treatable with the right medication. She said it was better it manifested while we were still in India than later in Nigeria, for only then would she be worried. She advised us to go back to the Emirates Airlines office and reschedule our flight for another two weeks.

The following day, Aunty Adeline called to tell us that we were in the local news in Anambra State and also a testimony in the local churches. We thanked the Lord once more for his faithfulness.

Later that night, Dike walked round the apartment carrying his bath bucket till he became very tired and sleepy at about 10pm. He began to grunt in his sleep and at 11pm I tried to reposition him, only to discover he was warm to the touch. I took his temperature and it was 100.3 degrees Fahrenheit. I sent an SMS to Dr. Neelam around 1am and she asked me to tepid sponge him and give paracetamol syrup. I monitored him all through the night; his temperature rose to 104.3f by early morning and at about 11am, the fever broke but he was very weak and still grunting. We took him to the hospital and met with Dr. Rajeev who took some blood samples.

Later that day, he was admitted in hospital because his oxygen circulation measured 91.2 and I was told that if it went below 90, it would be critical. His urea level was very high for he had not drunk much water all day. However his echo, chest x-ray and ECG were fine.

The Open Heavens text for Sunday the 20th of September 2009 was titled "Blending Gaze and Expectation" with the text from Psalm 121: 1-8. The message stated that if you are expecting help from above but looking sideways at those you know, you will not know when your help will be delivered. We are to look unto God and not unto man. The memory verse was James 1:17.

> "Every good gift and every perfect gift is from above and cometh down from the Father of lights with whom is no variableness, neither shadow of turning."
> James 1:17

As the days progressed, the messages from the devotional continued to give me the assurance that the Lord was in total control of our situation and our future was in His hands.

The reading of the 23rd of September 2009 in The Word for Today was titled "Good works…God prepared in advance for us" with text taken from Ephesians 2:10. The message read that anytime we ask "What on earth are we here for?" the answer in the Bible remains: 'To do good works which the Lord prepared in advance for us to do".

The one who trusts in God is compared to a tree planted by the riverside. The action point said: Those who dare to trust God to the point of foolishness ultimately end up as winners.

Going Home

We eventually left New Delhi on the 7th of October 2009 and arrived in Abuja the next day which was Amaka's birthday, just in time to celebrate with her. We were received into the warm embrace of our family and friends, as Chinenye who dutifully stayed with the children all through my stay away from home, had planned a party for Amaka's birthday and a surprise reception for all to receive us. Only Mike and Chinenye had known of our return date, so the children were overjoyed to receive us. I would reckon our return was the best birthday gift Amaka had ever received.

There is no doubt that we took up our cross and from day to day, we journeyed serendipitously till we arrived home with our beloved son Diken'agha.

Almost nine years later, after numerous unaccounted travails, euphoria, anxiety, journeys both for medical check-ups and for leisure, we stand to testify that it was more than a miracle celebrating the life of Diken'agha, Kenechukwu, Nadim, Yobanna, Victory, Miracle Ezeanya for indeed, all about him was certainly more than a miracle.

Afterwards

Nadim
You came to me when I least expected you
A child of destiny you proved to be

I had disputed the doctor's diagnosis
I was convinced I was sick
But my theory proved a fallacy
Then I became amused and excited
Even choosing a date for your birth
Alas
You came on another day
Ordained for you by our Lord

Amazed
All about you became coincidental
As I realised it was all destined
Then
The challenge emerged
But you were a survivor
I became convinced after the battle with NEC
That you had come for a cause
Behold
Another challenge emerged
A little defect with a most alarming prognosis

You remained anaemic
And jaundiced from eye to skin
The battle line had been drawn
Your abdomen stretched and the itching set in
With the controversies emerging back home
You became an enigma
But
At the *nadir* of your life
God sent an angel to show the path

That led us to the doctor
Sankanararayan at Child Trust

For another six months
We went back home and then
To God's own country
And back again to India
In search of a medical solution
We mingled with the natives
Commuting on three wheelers
Attending vespers in the cathedral
You were my marsupial
As I carried you on my kangaroo pouch
From the hotel room to Sir Ganga Ram

Tiny as you were
With an incredible will to survive
Dr Neelam Mohan had high hopes for you
As we connected from the onset
She and I
Working together in spirit
To achieve the impossible
With God as our ally

Having destined you for success
I was surrounded by God's peace
And an unshakeable faith in Him
Despite the down times
I was filled with joy
Knowing victory would come at last

As I had caught the vision
I stood on the word of God
Firmly holding unto His promises
Having an unflinching faith
That your tomorrow will be alright
The Lord gave His grace
As the doctors' report manifested
With each test worse than the former
But
We believed the heavenly report
And as the pathologist's prognosis remained
Contrary to the strength you displayed
You became a maverick
And all were awed by you
Yet
We waited against all odds
But God had a plan on course
He brought forth the donors

Haresh and Preeya Ahuja
God matched the organs Himself
I was convinced you would be all right
The wait was worth the while
I had internal peace
I was ready to be martyred
You emerged the hero
The news broke in the media
You were an alien
Yet
You were celebrated

Dr. Soin and his team
They called you a miracle
Indeed you were
Your name appeared on Google
You had become a legend
For God ordained it
The Lord's peace engulfed me

I held unto the scripture
"Before I formed thee in the belly
I knew thee
And before thou camest forth
Out of the womb
I sanctified thee
And I ordained thee
A prophet unto the nations".

Diken'agha as I watch you run around
As I watch you sing to the Lord
As I watch you play your drums
And as I watch you ride your bike
With your helmet on your head
I am filled with peace and joy
My mouth is filled with praises
For its been a long long journey
Eyes have not seen
And ears have not yet heard
The great things God predestined for you

We praise God for you and
We dedicate you to his call.

And the peace of God
Which passeth all understanding
Shall keep your heart and mind
Through Christ Jesus

.... Chinwe Ezeanya

At the heart of Motherhood is endless patience –

For kids, tying shoe laces, spreading peanut butter, brushing their teeth.

When a mum really wants to yell, "Hurry up," she learns to smile and says instead, "Great job. You did it!"

....Laurie Monsees

BIBLIOGRAPHY

1. Achebe, C. Things Fall Apart. 1958. Heinmann Ltd. UK.
2. Adeboye, E. A. Open Heavens: A Daily Guide to Close Fellowship with God. Vol 8. Lagos. Tie Communications. 2008.
3. Adeboye, E. A. Open Heavens: A Daily Guide to Close Fellowship with God. Vol 9. Lagos. Tie Communications. 2009.
4. Ahmed, P.A. et.al. Pattern of liver diseases among children attending the National Hospital Abuja, Nigeria. Niger J Paed 2016; 43 (1): 46 – 50
5. Beaufoy, S. The SlumDog Millionaire 2008. Drama set in India. Produced by Christian Colson
6. Defflid (@defflid) l Twitter.com
7. Dike Ezeanya: First-cross liver transplant in India a success. The Virtual Dimension August 20, 2009. Retrieved from https://menontalks.wordpress.com
8. Dike Ezeanya Foundation for Liver Diseases and other Ailments. Retrieved from www.facebook.com.
9. Domino Effect: Two Toddlers Cured with one donor liver. Retrieved from theindianexpress.com>cities> Delhi. Jan 31, 2009.

(Story of Siya and Shaurya's. First Domino Liver Transplant.)

10. Ezeanya C. Song of Nadim. 2010. Oyster St. Iyke. Lagos.
11. First Domino Liver Transplant – India Book of Records. April 11, 2001. Retrieved from https://indiabookofrecords.in
12. India's first successful swap liver transplant 19 Aug. 2009. Retrieved from https://zeenews.india.com.
13. Kauffman, W. Safe Blood Africa Project. Global Network for Blood Donation, a Rotarian Action. Retrieved from https://ourblooddrive.org>stories>safe-blood-
14. Mbulela. Nigerian Infant, Indian in first swap liver transplants Nairaland Aug. 27, 2009. Retrieved from www.nairaland.com
15. Mohan, N. India's leading pediatric liver transplant specialist. Retrieved from drneelammohan.com
16. Nigerian Infant, Indian in swap liver transplant – Times of India 20 Aug 2009. Retrieved from https://m.timesofindia.com
17. Ogbonnaya, R. Nigeria: Liver Swap Surgery... How Doctors Saved Two Lives. 10 Sept. 2009. Retrieved from https://allafrica.com
18. Philbrick, R. Freak the Mighty. Drama film / 1998. Retrieved from https://Freakthemighty.wikia.com>wiki
19. Pryor, J. At the Heart of Motherhood. 2003: Hallmark Gift Books.
20. Ravi, K. R. 10 Munites to Creativity: Better Yourself Books, 2007.
21. Sharma, R. The Monk Who Sold His Ferrari: A fable about fulfilling your dreams and reaching your destiny. 2007. Mumbai: Jaico Books.
22. Sharma, R. Who will Cry When You Die. 2009. Mumbai: Jaico Books.

23. Sir Ganga-Ram Hospital New-Delhi. Retrieved from https://www.sgrh.com
24. Soin, A. S. Retrieved from www.logintohealth.com/arvinder_soin.
25. The Taj Mahal. Retrieved from https://www.tajmahal.org.uk>taj-mahal.

MEDICAL REFERENCES AND GAUGES

ALT/SGPT	0.60 IU/L
AST/SGOT	0.42 IU/L
Ammonia	7 – 35 umol/L
Bilirubin (Total)	.21 – 1 mg/dL
Bilirubin (Direct)	0 - .2 mg/dL
Alkaline Phosphates	117 390 IU/L
Total Protein	6.6 – 8.7 gm/dL
Albumin	3.5 – 5 gm/dL
Gamma Glutamyl Transferase (GGT)	0 – 64 IU/L
Tacrolimus	5 – 20 mg/mL
Hemoglobin	11.1 – 14 – 1g/dL
APPT (Active Partial Thromboplastin Time)	25 -34.2 (sec)

Platelete Count	200 – 450 thous/ul
NASBA (CMV)	
S – Creatinine	.6 – 1.3 mg/dL

Note: there are different reference gauges and terminologies for these tests but these are some of the regular tests Dike was subjected to amongst many others.

APPENDIX FOR PICTURES

Dike and Chinwe

Dike in his school uniform

Some of the surgical team at Sir Ganga Ram with the swap transplant four sitting – Haresh, Dike, Chi and Priya.

Standing on left – Dr. A.S Soin, Middle – Dr. Neelam Mohan, Right – Dr. Sonjir Sagey (Priya's doctor), Dr. Sanjiv Saigal (Hepatologist-Gold Medalist)

Dr. A.S Soin, Chinwe, Dike and Dr. Neelam

Dr Neelam Mohan and Dike at the Media Conference in New-Delhi on 19th Aug 2009